POINT OF NO RETURN

 Random House · New York

Point of No Return

by PAUL OSBORN

Based on the Novel by JOHN P. MARQUAND

Photographs by John Swope

For

MILLICENT AND JUDITH

Point of No Return was produced by Leland Hayward at the Alvin Theatre, New York City, on the night of December 13, 1951, with the following cast:

[In Order of Appearance]

EVELYN GRAY	*Susan Harris*
NANCY GRAY	*Leora Dana*
BILL GRAY	*Keith Russell*
CHARLES GRAY	*Henry Fonda*
JOE	*James Jolley*
FIRST TELLER	*Gene O'Donnell*
FIRST CLERK	*Stanley Tackney*
SECOND CLERK	*Heywood Hale Broun*
SECOND TELLER	*Davis Roberts*
MISS MARBLE	*Madeleine King*
MISS DINGLE	*Katherine Hynes*
ROGER BLAKESLEY	*Bartlett Robinson*
ANTHONY BURTON	*Frank Conroy*
MALCOLM BRYANT	*Robert Ross*
CONDUCTOR	*James MacDonald*
JACKIE MASON	*Phil Arthur*
JESSICA LOVELL	*Patricia Smith*
LAURENCE LOVELL	*Colin Keith-Johnston*
JOHN GRAY	*John Cromwell*
ESTHER GRAY	*Frances Bavier*
TAILOR	*Pitt Herbert*
MRS. BURTON	*Madeleine Clive*
MAID	*Harriet Selby*

Clerks, Tellers, Secretaries and Customers

Directed by H. C. Potter

Settings and Lighting by Jo Mielziner

Costumes Designed by Main Bocher

Assistant to Costume Designer—Frank Spencer

ACT ONE

Time: The Present

Scene I—The living room of Charles and Nancy Gray in Sycamore Park, Connecticut.

Scene II—The Stuyvesant Bank, New York City.

Scene III—Same as Scene I.

ACT TWO

On the way to Clyde.
Clyde, Massachusetts, 1929.
On the way back from Clyde.

ACT THREE

Same as Act One, Scene I.

ACT ONE

ACT ONE

Scene I

The living room of NANCY *and* CHARLES GRAY. *It is a typical suburban-style room, rather conventional. On a wall there is a painting of a three-masted ship in full sail. A card table is set up with breakfast things.*

As the curtain rises, EVELYN GRAY, *age eleven, is just sitting in a chair at right. She has her head buried in a geography book.*

NANCY'S VOICE
(Calling, offstage)

Bill—Evelyn—
    (NANCY GRAY *enters hurriedly from left. She is carrying a bowl of cereal.)*

NANCY
(Calling)

Evie! *(She looks up and sees* EVELYN*)* Oh! I didn't know you were down, Evie. Good morning.

EVELYN

Good morning.

NANCY

Well, can't you look up at me to say good morning, darling?

EVELYN
(Looking up)

Good morn— *(She stops as she notices the card table)* What are we eating in here for?

3

NANCY

Change. Variation. Besides the man is coming to wax the dining-room floor. (*She calls*) Bill!

BILL'S VOICE
(*Offstage*)

Coming!

EVELYN

Where's Mary?

NANCY

She went to spend the night with her sister in Brooklyn. She won't be back until tomorrow afternoon.—Bill!

BILL

Here I am.
(BILL *enters. He is thirteen. He starts to cross the stage, obviously on the way to the dining room. He does not look up, intent on working his yo-yo. He carries a magazine.*)

NANCY

Now hurry, darling, and get at your breakfast. The car will be here and you won't be finished. (*As* BILL *continues through the room, not looking up*) Bill!

BILL
(*Looking up and around*)
What are we eating in here for?

NANCY

Change. Variation. Besides the man's coming to wax the dining-room floor.

BILL

Where's Mary?

NANCY

She went to spend the night with her sister in Brooklyn. She won't be back until tomorrow afternoon. Is your father up yet?

BILL

He's in the bathroom. (*To* EVELYN) Will you pass the sugar?

EVELYN

Please.

BILL

I don't have to say please to you.

EVELYN

You do, too! Doesn't he, Mother?

NANCY

All right, say please, Bill. It won't hurt you.

BILL

Will you please, kindly, and with alacrity, please pass the sugar, please. (*As* EVELYN *smiles*) And don't look cute while you're doing it.

EVELYN

Mother!

NANCY

All right, now stop it, both of you! Evelyn, pass him the sugar and get on with your cereal.

BILL

Is Dad really going away tomorrow?

NANCY

(*With a slightly mocking air*)

He's going to Massachusetts—dear old Clyde, Massachusetts—the scene of his childhood.

BILL

Why is it?

NANCY

Because he was *born* there, darling. Born and brought up.

BILL

Why is he going back?

NANCY

Oh, just business of some kind. Now get on with your breakfast.

EVELYN

(*Who has looked it up in her book*)

"Massachusetts—Area—seven-nine-zero-seven square miles. Population — four-three-one-six-seven-two-one. Capital — Boston." It doesn't say anything about Clyde.

NANCY

Oh, it wouldn't, darling. Clyde is just a very *little* town—outside of Boston. Very pretty—very old—*very* very New England.

BILL

How long will Dad be gone?

NANCY

Oh, a long, long time. A whole day or two. We'll just have
to struggle along without him. We probably won't even recognize him when he comes back. He'll have to get to know you
children all over again, of course . . .

EVELYN

What are you talking about? You said he'd only be away
for a day or two.

BILL

Oh, turn off your motor. Don't you know when Mother's
being funny?

NANCY

Oh, I'm a funny woman.
(CHARLES GRAY *enters, newspaper in hand.*)

CHARLES

Good morning, everybody.

NANCY

Good morning, darling.
(*They kiss.*)

CHARLES

What are we eating in here for?

NANCY

Change. Variation. Besides the man's coming to wax the
dining-room floor.

CHARLES

Oh. 'Morning, Evie.

EVELYN

'Morning, Dad.

CHARLES

'Morning, son.

BILL

'Morning, Dad.

CHARLES
(*Sitting*)

Where's Mary?

NANCY

She went to spend the night with her sister in Brooklyn. She won't be back until tomorrow afternoon.

CHARLES

Are you sure she's *coming* back?

NANCY

Oh, yes. She's left everything in her room.

CHARLES

Thank God.
(*He passes his hand over his forehead.*)

NANCY

Headache?

CHARLES

A little.

NANCY

I'm sorry, darling.

CHARLES

It's just that we stayed out so late.

NANCY

Now, darling, who was it wanted to go to the Cliffords'? They had us in January and we had them and everything was square and now . . .

CHARLES

. . . we'll have to have them again. I know. Round and round.

NANCY

That's the way it is. How would you like your eggs?

CHARLES

Oh, boiled, for a change, I guess.

NANCY

Three minutes?

CHARLES

I never know what that means exactly.

NANCY

It means you let the eggs boil for three minutes.

CHARLES

I know *that!* I just mean what does it do to the egg? I don't like them too hard so you have to dig for them—but I don't like them so soft that all that sticky, watery stuff gets all over you.

BILL

Albumen.

CHARLES

What?

BILL

That's the name for the white of an egg.

CHARLES

Oh. (*To* NANCY) Well, just see that the albumen knows its place.

NANCY

I'd better make it four.
   (*She goes.* CHARLES *thinks a moment.*)

CHARLES

Bill—how do you pronounce f-o-l-k?

BILL

Folk.

CHARLES

How do you pronounce j-o-k-e?

BILL

Joke.

CHARLES

How do you pronounce the white of an egg?

BILL

Yolk.

CHARLES

Thought you just said it was albumen.
(*He laughs.*)

EVELYN

"The llama and the alpaca have never been raised success-
fully anywhere except by the Indians on the high slopes of
the Andes."

CHARLES

Really? That's a handy piece of information to have, Evelyn.
What are you studying?

EVELYN

My geography.

CHARLES

Your geography! Five minutes before you have to leave? Is
that the way you do your homework?

EVELYN

Um-hum. Some of it.

CHARLES

I assure you, Evelyn, you'll never get anything accomplished
in little snatches like that. (*To* BILL) Bill, you see that book
sticking out there? Bring it to me. (BILL *does so*) You see this
book?

EVELYN

Yes.

CHARLES

This is Boswell's *Life of Johnson*. I have intended reading it all my life. My father loved it. In fact, this was his own copy. Some time ago I decided to spend thirty minutes a day reading it. On the train to town. Do you know how much I remember of it?

EVELYN

How much?

CHARLES

"Parnassus has its flowers of transient fragrance, as well as its oaks of towering height, and its laurels of eternal verdure."

EVELYN

What does that mean?

CHARLES

I have no idea. Yet that's all I remember. Thirty minutes' reading a day will not materially improve your cultural deficiencies.

EVELYN

What does *that* mean?

CHARLES

It means you can't learn any geography by reading it five minutes before your school bus comes for you.

EVELYN

It's not the school bus. It's the school car. Why do you call it a bus?

CHARLES

Because it ought to be a bus. You kids ought to be going to a public school.

BILL
(*Closing his magazine*)
If we did get a boat, where would we keep it?

CHARLES
What?

BILL
(*Alarmed—shouting*)
The boat! The boat!

CHARLES
Now don't shout!

BILL
Yesterday you said it was about time you taught me to sail.

CHARLES
Oh, did I?

BILL
(*Excited*)
You haven't forgotten? You said since we live right here near the water we should have an eighteen-foot knockabout or something . . . You haven't forgotten?

CHARLES
No, no, of course not. Well, we'll think about it.

BILL
I don't see how you could forget a thing like that! You said . . .

CHARLES

Yes, yes, I remember, Bill. Don't shout! Put your magazine away and finish your breakfast. As a matter of fact, my father was always talking about getting me a boat, but he never did.

BILL

It's not hereditary, is it?

CHARLES

No, no, it isn't. (*The car horn is heard*) Now there's your bus—your *car,* I mean. (*The children begin to gulp their food.* CHARLES *gazes at them a moment in dismay, then calls*) Nancy!

NANCY
(*Rushing in*)

All right, children, come on. Last time we kept them waiting.

EVELYN

'Bye, Dad.

CHARLES

'Bye, Evie.

BILL

We'll talk about the boat some more tonight, eh, Dad?

CHARLES

All right, Bill.

NANCY

Come *on,* Bill!

(NANCY *and the children go off in a scramble. We hear their voices offstage.* CHARLES *sighs his relief and looks at his paper. In a moment,* NANCY *returns.*)

You know, we're awfully smart, getting up this twenty
minutes earlier. Now we don't have to rush any more and
we've time to eat for a minute before we have to go to the
station and . . . (*She sits by* CHARLES) That suit looks nice.
The cleaners did a good job on it.

CHARLES

A little too much benzine for my taste.

NANCY

That'll wear off by the time you get to the bank. Oh, you've
forgotten your handkerchief, though.

CHARLES

Never mind the handkerchief. I'm not running for any
office.

NANCY

Oh, yes, you are, darling! And don't you keep forgetting
it! You're right in there polishing apples.

CHARLES

All right, Nancy.

NANCY

What's the matter? You are in there polishing apples,
aren't you?

CHARLES

I suppose I am, damn it. I suppose I've spent most of my
life polishing one apple or another. If you have to earn a
living, life is a series of apples. But I don't like to be reminded
of it.

NANCY

Sorry. Oh, by the way, don't forget to put two hundred dollars in the housekeeping account. It's down to twenty and I'm going to draw on it again today.

CHARLES

Down to twenty? How'd it get down there?

NANCY

It just sank and sank.

CHARLES

We have the most eccentric sinking fund. . . . All right, Nancy.
(*A moment's pause.*)

NANCY

Charley, I've been thinking. If you're going to Clyde tomorrow, you'll be back by Thursday, won't you?

CHARLES

Thursday or Friday morning.

NANCY

How about asking the Burtons for dinner Friday night?

CHARLES

Nancy! You know we can't ask the Burtons!

NANCY

I don't see why not.

CHARLES

Because it would be too obvious.

NANCY

The Blakesleys are going to ask them. Molly told me.

CHARLES

If the Blakesleys want to creep to Anthony Burton, let them. I'm damned if I will.

NANCY

Well, if Burton gives that job to Roger Blakesley rather than to you . . .

CHARLES

Oh, Roger's a good man. Don't underestimate Roger.

NANCY

You'd never for a minute be worried about Roger Blakesley if you hadn't taken time out to go to the war—when Roger used that time to dig himself in solid—because you're twice the man that Roger Blakesley is.

CHARLES

You think so?

NANCY

You know you are, darling. Charley, why don't you ask Burton today how it stands? Tell him you can't sleep . . . Oh, I heard you tossing around last night. Tell him that if Roger Blakesley is going to get the job—well, at least you want to *know*. You might even tell him how they're making bets in the washroom as to whether you or Roger—all the clerks standing around in there . . .

CHARLES

I don't want to tell him that. It's embarrassing.

NANCY

Burton's the president of the bank. He doesn't know everything that goes on. He hates anything that makes the bank look undignified. After all, he's the one who is always saying banking is an "art."

CHARLES

Just how do you think I should open my remarks?

NANCY

You could say, "Look, Tony, everybody knows that you're considering either Blakesley or me for this vice-president vacancy. Now I've been around here long enough. Of course, I was out during the war and Roger wasn't . . ."

CHARLES

Nancy! That's the most unscrupulous . . .

NANCY

Yes—yes—all right—you don't have to mention that Roger wasn't. He knows that anyway.

CHARLES

Look, Nancy, I'm not going to mention anything. Have you any conception of what would happen if I said all that to Tony?

NANCY

Well, you'd know where you stood.

CHARLES

I certainly would.

NANCY

Well, maybe I got carried away a little?

CHARLES

You got carried away a lot.

NANCY

All right. But if you want to be an assistant vice-president all your life and sit at that desk that's not even on the carpet . . .

CHARLES

I don't. I'd like to be a big *vice*-president and sit at one of those big desks right up there solidly *on* the carpet, but I'm damned if I'm going to creep to it.

NANCY

And it would be "creeping" if you ask the Burtons here for dinner Friday?

CHARLES

It would. It most decidedly would.

NANCY

Okay, darling. Okay.

CHARLES

Okay. (*They sit a moment in silence.* CHARLES *looks up at her, sorry*) Nancy, is it going to break your heart if I don't get the job? Because I may not get it, you know.

NANCY

I know. But we can hope. In fact, I had a dream last night. I dreamed today was the day.

CHARLES

What day?

NANCY

The day! About the job!

CHARLES

Well, did you dream I got it or did Roger Blakesley get it?

NANCY

You got it, silly. It was a dream, not a nightmare.

CHARLES

I hope you're right, Nance.

NANCY

You walked into the bank—it didn't seem any different from any other day—but after a few minutes Tony Burton came in and he called you over to his desk and he said, "Sit down, Charley. Now about this vice-president vacancy—it's yours."

CHARLES

What did I say?

NANCY

Oh, my God, I don't remember!

CHARLES

That's important! I took it, didn't I?

NANCY

Oh, you took it. You took it.

CHARLES

That's good.—Well, keep dreaming, Nance.
(*A moment's pause.*)

NANCY

Will you be taking the five-thirty home?

CHARLES

Yes, I suppose so.

NANCY

If you don't—call me.

CHARLES

I'll make it.

NANCY

We're going to the club for the dinner dance.

CHARLES

Oh, Lord, that's right. I'd forgotten.

NANCY

I thought maybe you had. (*Pause*) Why is it you're going to Clyde exactly?

CHARLES

I don't know the details yet. Some securities Tony wants me to look into. I once told him I was born and brought up in Clyde and he never forgets anything.

NANCY

I suppose you'll come back all—funny.
    (CHARLES *looks at her, sharply.*)

CHARLES

What do you mean by that?

NANCY

You always act funny even when you only *think* about Clyde.

CHARLES

I don't act funny. It's just that you always get edgy if I even speak about it. I don't see why either.

NANCY

You know perfectly well why. Clyde's full of queer, ingrown people—you said so yourself.

CHARLES

Well?

NANCY

And *you* always get queer and ingrown whenever you
speak about it.

CHARLES

Nonsense.
        (*A moment's pause.*)

NANCY

I suppose you'll run into a lot of people you used to know.

CHARLES

I doubt it. I'll be too busy. Besides, after twenty years I
probably wouldn't recognize them anyway.

NANCY

Of course you would. Jackie—. What's his name? The boy
who lived next door to you?

CHARLES

Jackie Mason.

NANCY

Jackie Mason. Then that Lovell girl—the one you wanted
to marry?
        (*A slight pause.*)

CHARLES

I won't be seeing Jessica Lovell.

NANCY

Oh, you can if you want to!

CHARLES

I know I can if I want to but I don't want to.
(*Pause. Suddenly* NANCY *shudders.*)

NANCY

I'd hate to go back to the place where I was brought up!
All those memories. People you have nothing in common with
any more. I bet you'll feel the same way. Don't let it get you
down, will you, darling?

CHARLES

As a matter of fact, I'm rather looking forward to it. Good
Lord, I haven't been back to Clyde since I left there—a good
twenty years ago.

NANCY

You won't like it.

CHARLES

I don't know. I'd sort of like to see our old house on Spruce
Street again. I'm curious to see whether I'd feel the same way
I did when my father was alive and we were all living there.
(*He pauses a moment*) I still can't help but feel my father
was a highly intelligent man. He must have known what the
odds were against him.

NANCY

That never stops anyone when he gets caught by it.

CHARLES

I was just thinking about him this morning. I suppose one

of the reasons I got started working in a bank was because he was so damn erratic. He scared me. I wanted something solid and secure. (*He looks at his watch, suddenly*) Oh, good Lord, now I've got to dash!

NANCY

Kiss me now so you won't have to at the station. (*They kiss.* CHARLES *hurries out for his coat, hat and brief case*) And Charley—I don't want to sound picky—but if you should get to thinking about it and decide to say anything to Mr. Burton about dinner Friday . . . (*Suddenly* CHARLES *laughs*) What's so funny?

CHARLES

The little woman kissing her husband good-bye. Everything depends on this moment. Get the job or Junior can't go to boarding school. And what about the next payment on the house? Good-bye, darling, don't come back without being the vice-president of the trust company.
(*Again he laughs.*)

NANCY

Don't say that!

CHARLES

Why not?

NANCY

Because maybe you're right.

CHARLES

Now wait a minute.

NANCY

Because if you say that—if you *mean* it—maybe it *isn't* much, but it's all we have. Maybe it isn't much, but then maybe we *aren't* much. And if you feel that way, there won't be *anything* any more.

(*She turns away to the sofa, near tears.*)

CHARLES

Nancy . . .

NANCY

If that's the way you feel . . .

CHARLES

Nancy, I'm not talking about you. I'm talking about the whole set-up.

NANCY

It's the set-up we're in.

CHARLES

I know it is, damn it.

NANCY

And I'm part of the set-up!

CHARLES

I'm talking about the whole picture. It's so damned . . . Look, Nancy, I've just *got* to go! I'll miss the train. I've only got . . . (NANCY *hurries out without answering*) Nancy—. (*He turns and picks up his brief case*) Damn! (*As he starts out after her*) Nancy!

BLACKOUT

(In the darkness we hear:)

CHARLES' VOICE

Hello. Hello, Operator. For Heaven's sake let's get together on this. I'm calling Sycamore Park, Connecticut, 827.

(The lights go up on a telephone booth at left. CHARLES *is at the phone. The lights go up on a telephone booth at right.* NANCY *enters as the phone rings. She picks it up.)*

NANCY

Hello.

CHARLES

Hello—Nancy?

NANCY

Charley? What's the matter? Where are you?

CHARLES

Grand Central. I just got in.

NANCY

(Mystified)

What's the matter? What's happened?

CHARLES

Nothing—nothing—I just thought I'd—er—call.

NANCY

Oh.

CHARLES

No reason.

NANCY
(*Quietly*)

I see.
   (*Slight pause.*)

CHARLES
(*At a loss*)

Er—get home all right?

NANCY

Fine.

CHARLES

Good. Well, I guess that's all. I just wanted to be sure
you . . .

NANCY

Charley?

CHARLES

What?

NANCY

Why did you call?

CHARLES

Oh, damn it all, Nancy, I hate to start off the day this way.
The way we did.

NANCY
(*Soberly*)

Me, too.

CHARLES

I didn't mean to be . . .

NANCY

Neither did I.

CHARLES

I got to thinking on the way down . . .

NANCY

So did I. On the way home . . .

CHARLES

And—(*he hesitates*)—look, I guess I can ask the Burtons to dinner if . . .

NANCY

Don't, darling, if it makes you feel lousy.

CHARLES

Well, it's just that . . .

NANCY

I know. Let's skip the Burtons.

CHARLES

(*With a sigh of relief*)

All right, fine. (*Slight pause*) What are you going to do all day?

NANCY

Oh, I'll find something.

CHARLES

Don't be too bored.

NANCY

Bored? Whatever made you think I was bored?

CHARLES

Well, out there all alone all day—nothing much to do . . .

NANCY

Nothing much to do! I'm running a home, Charley!

CHARLES
(*Hurriedly*)
Oh, sure, sure—I know—and it's a big job, too.

NANCY

Thanks. It *does* keep me busy at odd moments through the day. And then I *do* have the children later—that helps. Charley, I was thinking—on the way home—about your going to Clyde tomorrow. It's certainly a nasty time for you to have to be away—just when Tony's going to pass out that job any minute. Out of sight out of mind.

CHARLES

I know. I thought about that, too.

NANCY

Don't think Roger Blakesley won't make the most of it.

CHARLES

Well, there's nothing I can do about it.

NANCY

You might ask Burton if you could put off going for a week or so.

CHARLES

I *can't* ask him that, Nancy.

NANCY

No, I suppose not. I don't seem to be able to stop coaching from the sidelines, do I?

CHARLES

That's all right. That's natural.

NANCY

And maybe today is the day after all.

CHARLES

Maybe, Nance.

NANCY

I don't suppose there's any way you could call it to Burton's attention, though.

CHARLES
(*Right back where he was*)
No! No, there isn't.

NANCY
(*Hurriedly*)
No, no, of course not. All right, good-bye, darling.

CHARLES

Good-bye, Nancy.
(*They hang up.*)

BLACKOUT

ACT ONE

Scene II

The Stuyvesant Bank. One of the tellers enters and meets
JOE, *the doorman.*

JOE

Good morning, Mike.

TELLER

Good morning, Joe.

CLERK

Hey, Mike . . .

TELLER

Who do you want your money on today?

CLERK

Two on Blakesley.

TELLER
(*Surprised*)

Yesterday you were on Gray.

CLERK

Yeah, I know—but Mr. Burton had a long talk with
Blakesley yesterday and Blakesley acted in pretty good spirits
when he left.

31

TELLER

(*He moves away and approaches another clerk*)
How about it?

SECOND CLERK

Two on Blakesley.

TELLER

(*Worried*)
What's the idea? Everybody's turning to Blakesley.

SECOND CLERK

Old man had a long private talk with him yesterday.

TELLER

Guess maybe I got the wrong hunch here.

SECOND TELLER

(*Coming up*)
Mike . . .

FIRST TELLER

Yeah?

SECOND TELLER

Five on Gray!

FIRST TELLER

(*Brightening*)
Yeah?

SECOND TELLER

Sure. It's a cinch.

SECOND CLERK

Like hell it is.

SECOND TELLER

Just because the old man had a little talk with Blakesley doesn't mean anything.

SECOND CLERK

Hey, watch it!
(*They look up quickly and see that* ROGER BLAKESLEY *has entered.*)

JOE

Good morning, Mr. Blakesley.

ROGER

Good morning, Joe. Mr. Burton not in yet?

JOE

Not yet, Mr. Blakesley.
(BLAKESLEY *goes to his desk. His secretary,* MISS MARBLE, *is there.*)

MISS MARBLE

Good morning, Mr. Blakesley.

ROGER

Good morning, Miss Marble. Where are those papers on that Catlin thing Mr. Burton wanted me to look into?

MISS MARBLE

Right here, sir.
(*She hands him the papers and he studies them as* CHARLES *enters.*)

ROGER

Oh, good. Thank you.

JOE

Good morning, Mr. Gray.

CHARLES

How are you, Joe?

JOE

Fine, thanks.

CHARLES

Are you a grandfather yet?

JOE

Not yet, but any minute now.

CHARLES

Good. (*He starts toward his desk*) 'Morning, Roger.

ROGER

Hi, Charley. Missed you on the train.

CHARLES

No, I just made it. I didn't bother to come up to the car.

ROGER

I was just wondering about that Catlin business Tony wants us to look into. What do you think about it?

CHARLES

I think we ought to stay out of it. (CHARLES' *phone rings.* MISS MARBLE *answers*) But you and I ought to talk it over before we meet the attorneys. How about lunch?

ROGER

Boy, I just can't make it. I have a date with Tony at the University Club.

CHARLES

Oh. There's a lot more to banking than you think, isn't there?

ROGER

Banking is an art, isn't it?

MISS MARBLE

Mr. Gray . . .

CHARLES

Good morning, Miss Marble.

MISS MARBLE

It's Mrs. Whitaker.

CHARLES

(*Into telephone*)

This is Mr. Gray . . . Yes, I'll hold on.

MISS MARBLE

She's called twice already this morning.

CHARLES

Good morning, Mrs. Whitaker.—Oh, I feel fine, thanks. How do *you* feel?—Fine, fine—You have? Really? What kind is it?—A Pekingese!—Yes, I like dogs very much. What's its name?—Julie!—That's nice. Does she bite?—A hole in the rug, eh? That's terrible. Well, that's the trouble with having dogs in the city. Oh, yes, of course we have to excuse them a lot. After all, they're not human. (*He adds quickly*) Oh, I know, I know. I'm sure she's nearly human.—Practically speaks, eh?—Tonight? Why, yes, we were—At six-thirty? Why, no, I'd love to come out to your house at six-thirty, Mrs. Whitaker—No, it won't be inconvenient at all—All right—I'll look forward to talking to you and Julie both. Yes, that's right—All right, six-thirty, Mrs. Whitaker. Good-bye.

(CHARLES *hangs up as* MR. BURTON *enters.*)

BURTON

Good morning, Joe. That baby come yet?

JOE

Not yet. Expecting any minute.

BURTON

Good. (*He goes to* ROGER) Good morning, Roger.

ROGER

Good morning, Mr. Burton.

BURTON

Did you look into that Catlin matter?

ROGER

Oh, yes, I did. In my opinion, I don't think we ought to have any part of it.

BURTON

That's very sound judgment, Roger. I feel the same way about it. (*He stops by* CHARLES' *desk*) Good morning, Charles.

CHARLES

Good morning, Mr. Burton.

BURTON

Everything under control?

CHARLES

Mrs. Whitaker's been after me . . .

BURTON

Well, as long as she's after you and not me.

CHARLES

Oh, she's nice enough if you tell her what she wants to hear.

BURTON

You handle her very adroitly, Charles. By the way, did you get a chance to look over the Catlin papers?

CHARLES

Yes, I did.

BURTON

What do you think?

CHARLES

I think we ought to stay out of it.

BURTON

That's exactly what Roger and I feel. (CHARLES *smiles slightly*) Well— (*He nods and smiles and goes on toward his desk. Before getting there he turns*) Oh, I forgot, I'd like to see you, Charley. Would you come over? (CHARLES *sits a moment, wondering.* BURTON *goes into his office where his secretary is waiting*) Good morning, Miss Dingle.

MISS DINGLE

Good morning, Mr. Burton.
(CHARLES *comes in and stands.*)

BURTON

Sit down, Charley. I wanted to—oh, we'd better have Roger here. Miss Marble, will you ask Mr. Blakesley to step over here, please?

MISS MARBLE

Yes, Mr. Burton.
(*She goes to* BLAKESLEY.)

BURTON

How are Nancy and the children?

CHARLES

They're wonderful. They keep me out of trouble.

BURTON

Nancy's a fine girl. We ought to see more of her.

CHARLES

Well—she was saying—we ought to—to—(*He can't bring himself to say it*)—see more of you, too.

BURTON

Yes, we ought.
      (BLAKESLEY *comes in.*)

ROGER

Did you want me, Mr. Burton?

BURTON

Yes, sit down, Roger.

ROGER

New picture?
      (*He picks a photograph up from* BURTON's *desk.*)

BURTON
      (*Pleased*)

Yes—yes—my girls gave it to me.

ROGER

Say—look at that—pretty nice.

CHARLES
      (*Looking at it, lamely*)

Yes—pretty nice.

BURTON

Yes—yes, they're nice girls. Babs is at Sarah Lawrence now.

BLAKESLEY
      (*Intensely interested*)

Really!

CHARLES
(*Not to be outdone*)
You don't say!

BURTON
We miss her, of course, but then we telephone her every evening.

BLAKESLEY
(*Reading*)
"To America's most representative daddy, Gladys, Olivia, Babs." Intelligent-looking kids, Tony.

BURTON
Thank you. Well—let's get down to business. It's about your running up to Clyde, Charley. (*He picks up a sheaf of papers that he refers to now and then*) We have a new depositor who has applied for a six months' loan of three hundred thousand dollars. His name is Godfrey W. Eaton.

ROGER
You know him, don't you, Charley?

CHARLES
(*Thinking*)
No, I'm afraid not.

ROGER
No? He's at the Seneca Club. I met him playing golf. Everybody at the club knows Godfrey Eaton.

BURTON
Yes—it was very astute of you, Roger. (*To* CHARLES) Roger brought him in to us the other day.

CHARLES

I see.

BURTON

Miss Dingle, do you have that listing of Eaton's?

ROGER

Yes, I've seen quite a bit of Godfrey lately. I'm surprised
you never ran into him, Charley.

CHARLES

As a matter of fact, there're quite a few people I haven't
run into.

ROGER

You don't get around enough, feller. Why, I changed from
the Oak Knoll Club to the Seneca just to meet some new
people. But you can sweeten a lot of contacts that way, too.

BURTON
(*Reading*)

It seems Eaton is the head of a substantial tile manufactur-
ing company. He comes from the Middle West—owns a
number of small factories there. Part of the collateral is in
government bonds and part in stocks.

CHARLES

He sounds pretty safe.

BURTON

Yes, he does. Although we've got to be careful these days.

CHARLES

Of course, it's none of my business, but I wonder why he
didn't go to his own bank.

ROGER

Well, I guess that was my fault, Charley. I sort of talked him into it. I've been selling him on the personal service of small banks.

BURTON

He's also a director of the Pacific Investors Trust. But still, Charles has put his finger on something. No matter how persuasive you were, Roger, why should Eaton come around to us?

ROGER

Because he likes us. He told me he liked you, too, very much, Tony. (*He laughs lightly*) But then why shouldn't he? I like you too, Tony. That's why the Stuyvesant Bank is a great bank. Everybody likes Tony.

CHARLES

I'd love Tony if he'd lend me three hundred thousand dollars. That's the way it is. Love and money.
(*They all smile again, then* BURTON *becomes business-like.*)

BURTON

He's putting up enough. There's only one security I question. It's an unlisted company from Clyde, Massachusetts—the Nickerson Cordage Company—a block of five thousand shares at twenty dollars a share.

ROGER

I think you're right, Tony, that should be looked into.

BURTON

That's why I'm asking you to run up there, Charley, since you once lived there and know the background. Look things over. Talk to people. How are you planning to go? Take the midnight?

CHARLES

No. I thought I'd take a plane to Boston tomorrow morning—and then a train to Clyde— (*He breaks off suddenly*) Tony, is there any rush about this?
(ROGER *looks at him quickly. A moment's pause.*)

BURTON

How do you mean, Charles?

CHARLES

I mean, is there any reason I should go tomorrow? Would a week or so from now make any difference?

ROGER
(*Quickly*)

Well, it's certainly not too good to keep a man like Godfrey Eaton waiting.
(CHARLES *turns and faces him. They eye each other.*)

CHARLES

Why not? I imagine to a man like Eaton a few days wouldn't matter.

ROGER

I sort of had the feeling—well, that this ought to be finalized right now. Don't you think so, Tony?

BURTON

Have you any especial objections to going tomorrow, Charles?

(*A moment's pause.* ROGER *watches him.* CHARLES *throws it off.*)

CHARLES

No. Of course not. It *would* be better now.

(ROGER *is obviously relieved.*)

BURTON

Stay as long as you like and see if you can get some figures. As a matter of fact, I envy you getting away for a while. You're looking a little tired, Charles.

ROGER

(*Putting his hand on* CHARLES' *shoulder*)

I noticed that myself. You are looking a little tired, feller.

CHARLES

(*Laughing*)

Wouldn't you like to come along with me, Roger? Why don't you all come?

BURTON

(*Rising*)

I wish I could, for one. But I'm the representative daddy. Well, I see we're open.

CHARLES

Roger . . .

(CHARLES *and* ROGER *cross to their desks.*)

BURTON

Miss Dingle!

(BURTON *turns back to his desk. Waiting for* CHARLES *is* MALCOLM BRYANT, *a man of about fifty-two, whom we have previously seen enter the bank.*)

MALCOLM

Well, if it isn't Charley Gray.

CHARLES
(*Puzzled*)

Good morning . . .

MALCOLM

Charley, don't you remember me?

CHARLES
(*Groping*)

Why, yes, of course—I—

MALCOLM

Come on, I could tell you anywhere, Charley. The child is father of the man.

CHARLES

I just can't . . . Was it in the war?

MALCOLM

Longer ago than that. Over twenty years. My God, Charley, I'm Malcolm Bryant.

CHARLES
(*Staring at him*)

Good Lord—Malcolm Bryant. I should have known you right away. Sit down, Malcolm. Good Lord, isn't that odd—we were just talking about Clyde. How are you, Malcolm?

MALCOLM

I dropped in to cash a government check and the cashier asked me if I knew anyone in the bank who could identify me, and I came in here to look around and there, by God, was you.

CHARLES
(*He takes the check, initials it, and hands it to* JOE)
Joe, cash it, will you please?
(JOE *takes the check and goes out.*)

MALCOLM
(*Looking around*)
So here's where you've ended up! What are you, Charley, a vice-president?

CHARLES
(*Uncomfortable*)
Well, no, I'm an assistant vice-president at the moment.

MALCOLM
How's Jessica?

CHARLES
Jessica? Oh—I don't know. I haven't seen her for a long time.

MALCOLM
What? Didn't you marry Jessica Lovell?
CHARLES
No.

MALCOLM
You didn't? Why didn't you? What happened?
CHARLES
Well, it's a long story, Malcolm . . .

MALCOLM

But, my God, you and Jessica were head over heels in love with each other . . .

CHARLES
(*Uncomfortable*)
Look, Malcolm, this isn't really the time or place . . .

MALCOLM

Was it her father?

CHARLES
Partially her father . . . Lots of things happened that year in Clyde, you know, Malcolm.

MALCOLM

I'll never forget those few months I spent in Clyde. A ghost town. A vital sort of ghost town. You've seen my book on Clyde, haven't you?

CHARLES

No, I never saw it.

MALCOLM

You didn't? It's the best thing the foundation ever got out. Here, wait a minute . . . (*He bends down and opens his* brief case. CHARLES *looks around uncomfortably.* ROGER *is trying to hear what is going on.* MALCOLM *straightens up, a book in his hand*) I'm off on a trip and I usually take three or four copies along. It has an outline of my methods of research. Here, have one.

CHARLES

Why, thanks, Malcolm.

MALCOLM

Yankee Persepolis—that's what I call Clyde—Persepolis.

CHARLES

Why Persepolis?

MALCOLM

Where the Persians worshipped memories. I stopped off in Persia in thirty-five on my way to India. I was going there to study some dog worshippers. (MISS MARBLE, *overhearing him, gives a start*) Not for you, you wouldn't like it. (*He puts his hand on* CHARLES' *arm*) Wonderful to see you, Charley. I wish I knew everything that has happened to you since I used to know you.

CHARLES

That's a pretty tall order. Anyway I don't see why you'd want to know.

MALCOLM

Because I'm an anthropologist. Besides, I always liked you, Charley. And I'm interested in people academically.

CHARLES

Yes, people always were rather like guinea pigs to you. But I don't mind.

MALCOLM

I know you don't. That's why I always liked you. You've got a damn tough mind, Charley. When did you leave Clyde?

CHARLES

Oh, shortly after my father died.

MALCOLM

Then what?

CHARLES

Well, I'd been working in Boston . . .

MALCOLM

I know. What'd you do then?

CHARLES

Well, I met a man who asked me to look him up in New York. I did. I got a job here in the Stuyvesant, and I did well enough to hold it through the depression. I married a girl who worked downtown in a law office.

MALCOLM

That's right. That's your pattern. Children?

CHARLES

Two. And we bought a house in the suburbs.

MALCOLM

I know—Greenwich.

CHARLES

No.

MALCOLM

No?

CHARLES

Sycamore Park. It's not far from Greenwich though. And as a matter of fact I'm still paying for it. And right now there's a vice-president vacancy and it rests between me and that guy sitting behind me trying to hear what we're saying and he's got a tough mind, too. There! Does that answer everything?

(MALCOLM *laughs and* CHARLES *smiles.*)

MALCOLM

Do you love your wife?

CHARLES

I thought you'd ask that, and the answer is yes. I love my wife. I love my home and my children.

MALCOLM

I thought you would. You're essentially a monogamous type.

(JOE *has approached the desk.* CHARLES *looks up with relief and takes the money.*)

JOE

Here you are, Mr. Gray.

CHARLES

Thanks, Joe. (*He hands the money to* MALCOLM) Here is your wampum. You'd better count it.

MALCOLM

(*Putting it down on* CHARLES' *desk*)

It has less intrinsic value than shell money. It's symbolism. Well, I'd better get going. I'm on my way to New Guinea.

CHARLES

New Guinea?

MALCOLM

Yeah, for the Pacific Investigation Institute. They had to have an anthropologist. Walter Sykes was going—you know, Sykes at the Peabody who did that work on the Micronesians?

CHARLES

Well, I . . .

MALCOLM
(*Surprised*)

Don't know him?

CHARLES

I'm afraid not.

MALCOLM
(*Surprised*)

Really? I thought everyone knew him. Anyway, his kidneys gave out last week and so they went around to the Birch Foundation and the Birch found me. I'm not especially interested in going. The only thing that will be interesting is the circumcision rite.

CHARLES

My God, do they let strangers see things like that?

MALCOLM

It all depends on how you handle the head man. And head men are all about alike. You must have one here.

CHARLES

Yes—yes, we have . . . You know, Malcolm . . . (*He looks around and drops his voice*) I've never told this to anyone but—a year or two after you left Clyde I tried to look you up in New York.

MALCOLM

You did?

CHARLES
(*Nodding*)

But you weren't here. I was still sort of upset about everything at that time. I thought you might take me on one of those trips of yours. You'd offered to take me on that one to Afghanistan, you know.

MALCOLM

My God, I'd have taken you. That would have been funny.

CHARLES

Yes, it would have been. Well, you get a lot of queer ideas when you're that age.

MALCOLM

Yes, sir, I'd have taken you. And if I had you wouldn't be sitting here in this—whatever it is. It takes a lot of guts to be your type these days. Well, got to get going to New Guinea.
(*He holds out his hand*)
Good-bye, good luck, Charley. I'll look you up when I get back.

CHARLES

Good-bye, Malcolm. Give my love to the head man.

MALCOLM

Give mine to yours. So long.
(*He starts out, notices* MR. BURTON, *and giving* CHARLES *a glance points at him surreptitiously.* CHARLES *grins and nods.* MALCOLM *turns and goes out of the bank.*)
(*Slowly* CHARLES *sits down. He is very thoughtful. He looks up and sees* ROGER *watching him.* ROGER *looks away quickly. Suddenly* CHARLES *begins to think of something. A thoughtful frown comes to his brow.* MISS MARBLE *approaches his desk.*)

MISS MARBLE

Ready for me, Mr. Gray?
(CHARLES *comes to a decision.*)

CHARLES

Just a minute. (*He rises and goes to* BURTON's *desk.* BURTON *looks up*) Mr. Burton, could I speak to you for a moment?

BURTON

Yes, of course, Charley.

CHARLES

I was just wondering. Was it *your* idea that I go up to
Clyde on this matter?

BURTON

Well, I see what you mean, Charley. Roger *did* bring in
this Mr. Eaton. I suppose it's his responsibility—but he doesn't
know Clyde and . . .

CHARLES

What I wondered is—was it *your* idea that I go?

BURTON

Well, no, Charley. Now that you mention it, Roger suggested it. You know Clyde—and he thought you were looking a little tired—and thought it wouldn't hurt any for you
to get away from the bank for a day or two.

CHARLES

I see. Thank you. (*He starts to turn away, stops, and turns
back*) Er—one other thing—er—Nancy suggested asking you
whether—whether you and Mrs. Burton would like to come
and have dinner wtih us Friday night.

BURTON

Friday night? Why, yes, Charley, we'd like to very much.

CHARLES

Good. Nancy will call Mrs. Burton.
    (*He nods briskly and starts back to his desk,* ROGER'S
    eyes following him.)

BLACKOUT

(*In the darkness we hear the ringing of a telephone.
The lights go up on a telephone, right.* BILL *is there,
reading his magazine. He is also eating an apple. He
answers the phone.*)

BILL

Hello?—Yes—Okay . . . Hello?
(*The lights go up on the telephone booth, left.* CHARLES
is at the phone. He is in a hurry.)

CHARLES

Hello, Bill. Is your mother there?

BILL
(*Looking at the magazine*)
She's taking a bath. You're going to the club tonight.

CHARLES

I know. I want you to give her a message.

BILL

Anything you say.

CHARLES

Tell her I'm not going to be able to get home. I've got some
business I've got to attend to and I'll have to go straight to
the club.

BILL
(*Indifferently*)
Anything you say.

CHARLES

I may not be there until just time to take her home.

BILL
(*Reading his magazine*)
Um-huh.

CHARLES

Bill . . .

BILL

Um-huh.

CHARLES
(*Sharply*)

Bill!

BILL
(*Coming alive*)

What?

CHARLES

Are you listening to me?

BILL

Of course I am.

CHARLES

All right. Tell her I won't have time to dress—so the shock won't be too great.

BILL

Okay. Dad?

CHARLES

Yes, Bill?

BILL

Dad, you believe there's a God, don't you?

CHARLES
(*Confused*)

Why—yes—sure, Bill . . .

BILL

Then if there's a God there must be an after-life, too.

CHARLES

Yeah—I guess so, Bill—Now I've got to catch my . . .

BILL

Then if there's an after-life—well—when someone dies—he doesn't just—go into nothing, does he? I mean, he must be *somewhere*.

CHARLES

I guess that's right, Bill. If you're interested in the subject we'll discuss it when . . .

BILL

(*Dispirited*)

Okay, Dad. Skip it.

(CHARLES *is torn between running for his train and the feeling that this may be an important moment in* BILL's *life. He hesitates.*)

CHARLES

Look, son, these are very important matters. I don't want to seem . . . (*He hesitates*) Was there something *especially* that's disturbing you, Bill?

BILL

Well, I was just thinking this afternoon about your father—and I got to feeling sorry for him.

CHARLES

(*Puzzled*)

My father?

BILL

Yeah—that is, if he died—and if there *is* an after-life—I was thinking how terrible he must be feeling right now.

CHARLES

Why?

BILL

Because he never gave you that boat he promised you.

CHARLES
(*Shouting*)

Now, look, Bill!

BILL
(*Grinning*)

You don't want to get yourself in that spot, Dad.

CHARLES

All right, cut it out! Now you give your mother that message, see?

BILL
(*Looking at the magazine*)

And Dad—I found a beauty in a magazine. A second-hand Lightning, only eight hundred and fifty dollars.

CHARLES

Bill!

BILL
(*Swiftly*)

I'll leave it propped up on the table for you so you can see it when you get some from the club tonight. Okay, Dad?

CHARLES
(*Wearily*)

All right, Bill, all right. You see you're in bed before we get home, too.

BILL

Oh, sure. 'Bye, Dad.

CHARLES

'Bye, Bill.

BLACKOUT

ACT ONE

Scene III

The same as Scene I. That night.

In the darkness, we see the flicker of a portable television set and hear the sound of a horror picture—with appropriate gruesome organ accompaniment. BILL *and* EVELYN, *in their night clothes, sit watching it. There is no other light in the room.*

FIRST MAN

Now you lay there quiet and ain't nobody gonna hurt you.

SECOND MAN

Ah, give her the woiks, Spikey. You gettin' chicken?

FIRST MAN

Who's gettin' chicken? Put that ice pick away.

SECOND MAN

Look out, she's gettin' the gag loose.

FIRST MAN

You didn't tie it tight enough. If she screams now . . .
(Suddenly there is a piercing woman's scream.)

FIRST MAN

Stop, you goon. Put that hammer down.
(There is a pounding on the door. Men's voices shout.)

FIRST COP

Open up, there!

57

SECOND COP

Open in the name of the law!

(*Loud pounding, a scream, a pistol shot, a groan and— as the organ music swells, frighteningly, the headlights of an automobile can be seen through the window. Quickly* BILL *jumps into action,* EVELYN *doing the same. They switch off the television set and we hear them scrambling out of the room, lugging the set with them. After a moment,* NANCY *and* CHARLES *can be heard coming into the house.*)

NANCY
(*Offstage*)

Look out for the furniture.

CHARLES
(*Offstage*)

I thought they were going to wax the floor.

NANCY
(*Entering*)

Tomorrow, he says. (CHARLES *turns on the lights as he follows* NANCY *in*) I thought I heard—I'll take a look. (NANCY *exits in the direction the children have gone.*)

(*The light that* CHARLES *has turned on reveals* BILL'S *magazine propped up on the table, and on the chair beside it rests a large square of cardboard upon which* BILL *has printed in large letters the word "BOAT" and drawn an arrow pointing toward the magazine.* CHARLES *stops and grins when he sees it. He takes off his coat and throws it over the chair. He picks up the magazine, looks at the advertisement* BILL *has mentioned, and tears it out. As he puts it into his pocket he discovers the copy of* MALCOLM BRYANT'S *book that is also there. He*

*takes the book out, glances at it, and tosses it onto the
table.* NANCY *enters.*)

NANCY

Sound asleep. They're really very good, Charles.

CHARLES
(*Sitting*)

Um-hum.

NANCY

Tired?

CHARLES

Uh-huh. Not sleepy, though.

NANCY

I suppose we ought to go right up. We've got to go to the
airport in the morning. Do you want a glass of milk first?

CHARLES

Before we go to the airport or before we go up?

NANCY

Before we go up, silly.

CHARLES

No. Oh, these parties. Did you have a good time, Nancy?
(NANCY *sits on the sofa by him.*)

NANCY

Well, yes, in a sort of long-term way.

CHARLES

What do you mean, long-term way?

NANCY
(*Kicking off her shoes*)
You know. It's what I've told you before. I like feeling we belong somewhere. It's what I've always wanted.
(*She leans back in his arms.*)

CHARLES
Well, so do I. I guess everyone does.

NANCY
It isn't the same for a man. He always belongs much more than a woman, up to a certain point. A woman just has to tag along. It's nice, when she likes tagging.

CHARLES
Well, I'm glad you like it—but I don't see why.

NANCY
I'll tell you why. Because I'm married to a damn nice man.
(*They kiss.*)

CHARLES
Sorry I was late tonight. I had to go out and wet-nurse the Whitakers. They want to buy a ranch in Arizona for a hundred thousand dollars but they haven't anything to sell that shows a loss. They're all upset about it.

NANCY
Poor things. Did you put that two hundred dollars in the housekeeping account?

CHARLES
Yes. What's that got to do with it?

NANCY
I just wondered.

CHARLES
(*Casually*)

Oh, by the way, the Burtons are coming to dinner Friday night.

(NANCY *straightens up as though jerked by wires.*)

NANCY

Charley!

CHARLES
(*Grinning*)

Um-hum.

NANCY

Now start at the beginning and tell me everything. Exactly how did it happen? Don't leave anything out.

CHARLES
(*Laughing*)

Well, Tony and Roger and I were talking about this Clyde business. Roger was pressing it all sort of hard—and well, then another fellow came in to see me—Malcolm Bryant . . .

NANCY

Never mind about Malcolm Bryant.

CHARLES

Well, it was something he said got me thinking—something about knowing how to handle the head man. He's going to New Guinea and . . .

NANCY

Never mind about New *Guinea*.

CHARLES

Anyway, it suddenly occurred to me—why was *I* being sent to Clyde? It was Roger's deal. So I asked Tony whose idea it was for me to go . . .

NANCY
(*Furious*)

And it was Roger's!

CHARLES
(*Nodding*)

That's right.

NANCY

To get you out of the way for a couple of days right now at the crucial moment!

CHARLES

It kinda looked that way. Of course, Roger said he was worried about me. Thought I looked tired and a couple of days away from the bank . . .

NANCY

Well, of all the low-down, sneaky . . . You wait until I see Molly!

CHARLES
(*Starting up*)

Now don't you dare tell any of this to Molly!

NANCY

But it's contemptible! I'd like to have that Roger Blakesley and . . . What did you do?

CHARLES

Nothing. What was there to do?

NANCY

Didn't you tell Roger what you thought of him?

CHARLES

Now what would be the point of that?

NANCY

Well, I wish I'd been there! I'd have . . .

CHARLES

Oh, no, you wouldn't! You just think you would.

NANCY

Well, I loathe—I just utterly loathe Roger Blakesley now! And there he was smirking around the club tonight.

CHARLES

You know what he said to me?

NANCY

What?

CHARLES

"Charley, I hope we can all be friends no matter what happens."

NANCY

Oh, I hate him—and Molly, too! Incidentally, what were you talking to her about tonight?

CHARLES

You. She said you always look lovely in those simple little dresses you wear.

NANCY

Molly can go—peddle her papers, too! Well, go on. You asked Tony to come to dinner. How'd you do it? Tell me exactly what you said.

CHARLES
(Blankly)
I said will you come to dinner Friday night.

NANCY

And what did he say?

CHARLES

He said "Yes."

NANCY
(*Irritated*)

But how did he *act*? Was he pleased, was he excited?

CHARLES

He didn't fall off his chair or anything.

NANCY

Well, how did it come up?

CHARLES

I'd gone up to his desk to ask him why I was the one being
sent to Clyde.

NANCY
(*Impatiently*)

Did he realize that *you* knew that Roger had suggested
your going?

CHARLES

He must have. Why?

NANCY

Tony's no fool. If he realized that Roger was trying to put
a fast one over—And I bet you anything he *did!* That's wonderful.

CHARLES
(*Uncomfortably*)

Look—I didn't mean to get in any dig at Roger . . .

NANCY

(*Radiant*)

Mean it or not, darling, you did! You got in a genuine, honest, nasty dig! You were just exactly as contemptible as Roger himself! Oh, I'm proud of you! Now, let's see, does Tony like duck, do you know?

CHARLES

How the hell should I know if Tony likes duck!

NANCY

Listen, Charley, when you talk to him next see if you can steer the conversation around toward food a little.

CHARLES

Look, Nancy! Tony Burton is going to eat what we give him and like it! Will you please stop planning the menu now?
(*There is a pause.* NANCY *is cuddled against him. Each thinks his own thoughts. After a moment.*)

NANCY

Charley?

CHARLES

What?

NANCY

What will you do if he takes Roger?

CHARLES

Let's not think about it now, Nance.

NANCY

But we *are* thinking about it! Both of us. What will you do?

CHARLES

If they don't like you well enough to move you up, it's time to get out.

NANCY
(*Bursting out*)
It's so unfair! After years of work you become specialized, you get used to the ways of just one organization, you really become too old to start again in a new one.

CHARLES
Hey, wait a minute. I'm not so old.

NANCY
You've seen plenty of men your age looking for a job. Oh, if we'd only done something about investing for ourselves instead of for other people.

CHARLES
You don't do much of that, you know, Nancy, when you're working for a bank.

NANCY
And Bill and Evelyn growing up so fast.
(*A moment's pause. Suddenly* NANCY *clutches him, burying her face against him, sobbing softly.*)
Oh, Charley, we didn't used to be afraid!

CHARLES
Don't Nance, don't!

NANCY
Now it seems to me we're afraid of everything!

CHARLES
Maybe fear's what makes the world go round.

NANCY
(*Looking up at him, trying to smile*)
Not love? I used to hear it was love.

CHARLES

Everyone's afraid of something—afraid of living, dying . . .
Maybe it's better than being afraid of losing money. That's
the way it is with the boys downtown. Do you know what I
wish?

NANCY

What?

CHARLES

I wish we weren't always being pushed around. I'd like for
once in my life to be able to tell someone to go to hell.

NANCY

Darling, you have such expensive tastes. You'd better just
tell me to go to hell, if you want to, and let it go at that.

CHARLES

All right. But it's not the same thing.

NANCY

Anyway I'm awfully glad we're afraid of the same thing.
It's healthy to have things in common. I'm awfully glad we're
in the same boat, darling. (*She reaches up and kisses him, then
gets up*) I'm going to get myself a glass of milk—and then
I'm going up. Sure you won't have one?

CHARLES

All right. I will. Thanks.

> (NANCY *goes out left.* CHARLES *rises slowly, stretches, and
> again notices the book given him by* MALCOLM BRYANT.
> *He picks it up and starts to read it. Suddenly we see
> that he gets very interested. He reads it intently.*)

Why, the dirty . . . (*As he reads,* NANCY *comes in with two
glasses of milk*) Why, the *dirty*—!

NANCY

What is it?

CHARLES

Remember I said a fellow came in to see me today? Malcolm Bryant? He's an anthropologist. He came to Clyde—oh, when I lived there—to make a social survey of some kind.

NANCY

(*Handing him the glass of milk which he has put aside*) Don't you want your milk?

CHARLES

(*Taking the milk and in a moment setting it aside again, untouched*) Everybody invited him to their houses—told him everything —in fact were pretty nice to him.

NANCY

What do you mean a social survey?

CHARLES

Well—it's a study he made of Clyde—calls it a typical New England town—and (*He turns to the front of the book and reads*) he's written it all out—hasn't even bothered to disguise it so you won't know who he's talking about. Listen to this:

"It will be well to define the very definite social strata of this town, as follows:

There are three distinct social groups, the upper class, the middle class and the lower class—but each of these will be divided into thirds—so we have the upper-upper, the middle-upper, and the lower-upper; the same way with the middle class—the upper-middle, the middle-middle, and the lower-middle; and the same way with the lower class . . ."

NANCY
(*Laughing*)
"The upper-lower, the middle-lower and the lower-lower."

CHARLES
Now just get this. "Typical of a lower-upper family are the Henry Smiths—father, mother, son and daughter. (*He looks up at* NANCY) The ancestral motif is as marked in this group as it is in the *upper*-upper. The same importance is attached to the preservation of the heirloom and the decoration of the grave. Thus on a wall in the Smith home, hanging over the patriarchal chair is a jealously guarded primitive oil painting of a three-masted sailing vessel captained by the Smiths' ancestor, Jacob Smith."
(*He looks at* NANCY *and they both regard the painting on the wall.* NANCY *lets out an explosion of laughter.*)

NANCY
Good Lord, it's you! The Smith family is your family, Charley!

CHARLES
(*Angrily*)
I know damn well it is! And I remember the exact time when Malcolm asked about that picture and I remember my mother's taking the pains to explain it to him.

NANCY
What else does he say about you? Let's see—what are you— a *middle*-upper?

CHARLES
(*Grimly*)
A *lower*-upper. "Like other lower-upper families, they dwell on a side street, yet are received on Mason Street." He says Mason Street—that's Johnson Street, of course.

NANCY

That's where Jessica Lovell lived, isn't it?

CHARLES

That's right. "Mr. Smith"—that's my father, of course—
"is a member of the Sibley Club, but is not a member of the
Fortnightly Reading Club. An intellectual man, whose financial status varies with the stock market, he is free to indulge
his whims because he is not bound by the rigidity of the
upper-upper class. Therefore, he is able to enjoy his position
as captain of the Volunteer Fire Department, a pastime which
seems to afford him great amusement." It did, too. "His wife,
Mrs. Smith, was Miss Jones, a physician's daughter (middle-
upper). She runs their house in a lower-upper manner—
(CHARLES *winces*)—with the aid of one maid (middle-lower)
coming in daily from outside. The son Tom, a likable—" (*He
begins to mumble something unintelligible*) Ah, nuts!
(*He stops, disgusted.*)

NANCY

Don't mumble! I didn't get that. What about the son Tom?
That's you!

CHARLES

It's just too damn silly!

NANCY

(*Grabbing the book*)

It's fascinating. Let me have it.

CHARLES

Now, Nancy—Now cut it out, Nancy!

NANCY

(*Getting the book*)

"The son, Tom, a likable young graduate of Dartmouth."
(*She laughs*) My likable young graduate from Dartmouth.

CHARLES

All right, all right.

NANCY

"—is received by the upper-upper but is not a member of the committee for the Winter Assembly—" (*Sympathetically*) Ohh!—"He is, however, in a position to move by marriage to middle-upper, or possibly even *upper*-upper status!"

CHARLES

Come on, Nancy. Give it to me.
    (NANCY *has sobered down and seems suddenly very serious.*)

NANCY

No, I want to read it. "He is on friendly terms with the daughter of Mr. Johnson (upper-upper), though there is little prospect of more than friendship." (NANCY *pauses a moment*) That would be Jessica Lovell.

CHARLES

Nancy, don't—

NANCY

(*She doesn't look at* CHARLES)
"An upper-upper-class family may be typified by the Johnsons, who live on Mason Street in one of those fine, Federalist houses. The drawing room was consciously built to house its greatest treasure, a magnificent wallpaper from France. They call it, with modest humor, 'The Wallpaper Room.' This is all a fitting frame for the ritual of Clyde's upper-upper class. Mr. Johnson, the father of the daughter that Tom (lower-upper) is on friendly terms with, is a widower, descendant of shipowners in the late eighteenth century. Judith, his lovely only daughter, is eminently suited to give the family ritual an added charm. It would be a matter of marked interest if

Tom (lower-upper) should ever be able to bridge the gap between himself and—" (*She stops reading*) She must have been very beautiful, Jessica Lovell. You did love her a lot, didn't you, Charley?

CHARLES

Yes, I did. But that was twenty years ago.

NANCY

I know.

CHARLES

As far as I'm concerned, Jessica Lovell could be dead.

NANCY

Oh, no. She's always been terribly alive for you.

CHARLES

That's nonsense, Nancy.

NANCY

She did something to you. I don't know what. But she hurt you.

CHARLES

Of course she did, at the time. But it wasn't only Jessica. There were a lot of other things too . . .

NANCY

(*Suddenly*)

Oh, Charley, when you go up there to Clyde tomorrow—why don't you try to find out—find out what happened to you—get Jessica Lovell and Clyde out of your system once and for all.

CHARLES

All right, Nancy. Let's skip it now.

NANCY

(*With a sigh*)

All right. (*She rises*) Well, I'm going up. What are you
going to do? Sit up and worry about the bank?

CHARLES

No, I'm not. But I'm still not sleepy. I think I'll read awhile.
(*He picks up Yankee Persepolis.*)

NANCY

Because if you're going to worry we might as well do it
together.

CHARLES

I'm pretty well worried out tonight, Nancy. I'll just read.

NANCY

Don't be too long, will you? I won't be able to sleep till you
come up.

CHARLES

I won't.

NANCY

(*She hesitates a moment, then goes back to* CHARLES.)

Charley, are you sorry you married me?

CHARLES

Nancy, don't be . . .

NANCY

Are you sorry we had the children?

CHARLES

Of course not.

NANCY

Are you sorry you didn't marry . . .

CHARLES

Listen, Nancy. I love you, I love the children, now stop it. (*Slight pause.*)

NANCY

I'm going to miss you while you're gone.

CHARLES

I'll miss you. (NANCY *picks up her shoes and starts out again*) Oh, hell, wait a minute. I'll go up, too. I've got to get that plane in the morning. (*He picks up the book again*) That son-of-a-bitch.

NANCY

Who?

CHARLES

Malcolm Bryant. He might at least have made me a *middle-upper.*

(*He drops the book into the wastebasket and both of them go off.*)

Curtain

ACT TWO

ACT TWO

A day coach. It is an antiquated affair and it rocks and rumbles on the roadbed. It is rather chilly. It is late afternoon.

CHARLES GRAY *sits in one of the seats looking out of the window, rapt in sober, nostalgic contemplation of what he sees. He has on his hat and topcoat, the collar turned up.*

After a moment, the CONDUCTOR *comes by.*

CONDUCTOR

Tickets, please.

CHARLES
(Startled)
Oh—yes. (*He fumbles through his pockets and produces his ticket. As the* CONDUCTOR *tears it,* CHARLES *looks out of the window*) Isn't that Whiting's Creek out there?

CONDUCTOR

Yes, sir. Whiting's Creek.

CHARLES

It seems to me there used to be a—sort of little waterfall near here.

CONDUCTOR

Waterfall? (*He is puzzled. Then—*) Yes. Yes, there used to be a waterfall around here somewhere. But that was years ago.

CHARLES

Ah.

77

CONDUCTOR

They changed the creek to run around another way for some reason and that cut off the waterfall. (JACKIE MASON, *a man of about* CHARLES' *age, has entered and taken the seat in front of* CHARLES. *The* CONDUCTOR *passes on to him*) Tickets, please. Oh, yes, I got yours.

(*The* CONDUCTOR *goes off.* CHARLES *looks up casually, then looks back out the window, then suddenly turns again and looks at the back of the head before him. He frowns, and leaning forward peers over the shoulder of the man before him.* JACKIE, *feeling his stare, slowly turns around to face him.*)

CHARLES
(*His face lighting up*)

Jackie Mason!

(JACKIE *hesitates a bare moment, then starts scrambling to his feet.*)

JACKIE

Charley Gray!

CHARLES
(*With a broad grin*)

Jackie Mason! I knew it was you from the back of your head!

(*They shake hands excitedly.*)

JACKIE

Charley Gray! I can't believe it! Well, if it isn't Charley Gray!

CHARLES

I was just sitting there looking out at Whiting's Creek and I looked up and I recognized you from the back of your head!

(*They continue to pump each other's hands.*)

JACKIE

Well, what do you know! What are you doing here?

CHARLES

Just going to Clyde on business. Here, let's switch this around.

JACKIE

I've been in the smoker! Well, what do you know! (*They pull one seat around so that they can sit facing each other. They sit*) Charlie Gray! (*He slaps* CHARLES' *knee*) You don't look a day older, Charley!

CHARLES

You're looking fine, too, Jackie. Over twenty years . . .

JACKIE

I was just saying to Mother the other day—it still seems funny not to be able to go out in the back yard and yell for Charley to come over. Mother had a letter from your mother awhile back. Told us all about you. Married. Two kids.

CHARLES

That's right.

JACKIE

President of the Stuyvesant Bank.

CHARLES

I'm not the president, Jackie. In fact, I'm trying hard, at the moment, to become one of five vice-presidents.

JACKIE

You stick to it, Charley. You'll get there. You've got success written all over you.

CHARLES

Have I?

JACKIE

You sure have. Some difference! (*He laughs*) Remember in high school you used to say you didn't give a damn about getting on? Working, making money, meeting the right people? (*He laughs again*) Why, I remember you said once you wouldn't walk across the street to meet John D. Rockefeller.

CHARLES

Did I?

JACKIE

You sure did! Thought that was all nonsense. Oh, well, kid stuff! I guess you've met a lot of the right people now, all right.

CHARLES
(*Depressed*)

Yes, I suppose I have. (*Snapping out of it*) Well, how about you, Jackie? What have you been doing? Still at Wright-Sherwin?

JACKIE

Still there. In the accounting department.

CHARLES

Good.

JACKIE

Oh, it's nothing much—not like you, Charley.

CHARLES

What do you do?

JACKIE
(*Shyly*)

Well, matter of fact, I've been made the head of it.

CHARLES

No kidding! Well, you've certainly got where you wanted to get, Jackie.

JACKIE

Oh, I haven't done anything except in a small-town way.

CHARLES

I think you've done a helluva lot. Not married though?

JACKIE

No—no—

CHARLES

Well, don't give up, Jackie.
(*A moment's pause. They look at each other and smile.*)

JACKIE

(*Slapping* CHARLES' *knee again*)
Charley Gray!

CHARLES

That's me.

JACKIE

You don't look a day older, Charley.

CHARLES

You look fine, too, Jackie.

JACKIE

How long you going to be in Clyde?

CHARLES

Just a day or two.

JACKIE

Be taking this train back to Boston?

CHARLES

Yes.

JACKIE

Good. I'll see you. I've been having to go up to Boston all this week.

CHARLES

Oh, by the way, the reason I'm here is to find out about the Nickerson Cordage Company. What do you know about it?

JACKIE

Pretty sound, as far as I know.

CHARLES

I'm glad to hear it.

JACKIE

I can't get over it. It's a small world.

CHARLES

It sure is.

JACKIE

You know, I've been in New York a couple of times. Went past your bank once.

CHARLES

Why didn't you come in?

JACKIE

Well, I don't know. Didn't know for sure you'd be there. Pete MacDonald was with me. Boy, we sure had a time. We took New York apart.

CHARLES
(*Grinning*)

Yeah?

JACKIE

Yeah. Oh, we didn't really take it apart. We got awful drunk, though.

CHARLES

Well, that's the way it goes. (*Looking out the window*) My God, it all looks familiar. That's Brainard's Crossing, isn't it?

JACKIE
(*Glancing out*)

Yup.

CHARLES

Won't be long before we're in the tunnel now.

JACKIE

Nope. (*A moment's pause. JACKIE stirs uneasily*) Charley . . .

CHARLES

Yes?

JACKIE

I—well, I . . .
(*He stops.*)

CHARLES

What's on your mind, Jackie?

JACKIE

Well—(*He clears his throat*) It's about Jessica Lovell.

CHARLES

Oh, yes. I was going to ask you about her. How is Jessica?

JACKIE

Oh, she's very well. Very well and busy. She has the same interest in things, but then you know Jessica.

CHARLES

Well, I don't know her now. It's been a long time.

JACKIE

I don't want to bring up any painful memories.

CHARLES

Painful memories? (*He laughs*) Don't call them that, Jackie! They're too old. I'm glad to hear she's well and happy. She never married though, did she?

JACKIE

No—no, she didn't, Charley.

CHARLES

Her father?

JACKIE

No, I don't think it was entirely that. (*Slight pause*) I think she always hoped that . . .
(*He points to* CHARLES.)

CHARLES

Oh, nonsense! She knew I'd married, didn't she?

JACKIE

Yes. Jessica's a wonderful girl. She always wanted you to be happy. She's always wanted to hear about you. You see, Jessica had to talk to someone and I suppose I was elected. Just because you and I were such close friends. She still talks about you a lot.

CHARLES

Oh, come now! Maybe for a year or two after I left . . .

JACKIE

I wish you never had left, Charley. Of course I suppose you had to—with your father and all—it was pretty awful, the whole damn thing.

CHARLES

My God, Jackie, it's all been over for years.

JACKIE

But you know—there's something about women—I think that women stay in love longer than men—once they fall in love.—I think you ought to call on Jessica while you're here, Charley.

CHARLES

Oh, no, I couldn't, Jackie.—Here comes the tunnel.

BLACKOUT

(*In the darkness we hear:*)

CONDUCTOR'S VOICE

Clyde! Clyde! Kindly leave no articles in the car. Clyde! Station Clyde!

JACKIE'S VOICE

I hope you'll see her, Charley. Of course none of it was your fault. Nobody blames you at all. Just remember how she used to be. Sort of sad, you know, although she didn't show it much. So lonely until you came along. She's told me everything. She'll know you're here, Charley.

(*The noise of the train fades out, but the voices continue.*)

CHARLES' VOICE

My God, Jackie—you talk as if . . . Don't you realize this has been all over and done with for years? Look—I don't want to even think about it any more. That damned wallpaper room—I'll never forget the first time I saw it—the first time she took me home with her. We had to sneak into the house so we wouldn't wake the old man—I bumped into the damned furniture . . .

(*The lights have come up on:*)

(THE WALLPAPER ROOM, *and as we hear* CHARLES' VOICE *describing the scene we have seen* CHARLES *and* JESSICA *entering in the semi-darkness and* CHARLES *bumping into the furniture.* JESSICA *turns at the sound.*)

JESSICA
(*In a whisper*)

Did you bump yourself?

CHARLES

Ran into something very solid.

JESSICA

Stand still until I turn on the lights. We mustn't wake Father.

CHARLES

Don't you think it's too late for me to come in?

JESSICA

Of course if you don't want to . . .

CHARLES

I do want to, Jessica . . .

JESSICA

Well, then.

(*She turns on the lamp and suddenly the lights come up fully.* JESSICA LOVELL, *about twenty-one, straightens up and smiles at* CHARLES, *who is about twenty-four. He is rather stiff and embarrassed.*)

CHARLES

Good Lord!

JESSICA

We call this the "Wallpaper Room." I can't imagine why, can you?

CHARLES

Good Lord! That's certainly a lot of wallpaper.

JESSICA
(*Laughing*)

Oh, you get used to it. You know, it's really queer that you've never been in this house before.

CHARLES

There're a lot of houses in Clyde I've never been in.

JESSICA

I mean it's queer *now*. Would you like some cold root beer?

CHARLES

Not very much. Would you?

JESSICA

Not very much. (*They both laugh and sit*) In fact, it's rather queer we've hardly seen each other before. Both of us living in Clyde all our lives.

CHARLES

You've been away so much.

JESSICA

Yes, that's right. I've been away so much. Ever since I was fourteen, Father's taken me to Maine for the summers. And then at school at Westover and then Vassar. Were you ever at Vassar, Charley?

CHARLES

No, I went to Dartmouth.

JESSICA

No, I mean—oh, you know what I mean . . . But now I'm really back in Clyde.

CHARLES

I'm glad.

JESSICA

Are you? Oh, I wish I'd gone to school here—with all those people you know so well—then I wouldn't feel so far away and I wouldn't have worn this damn dress tonight. Why didn't you tell me it wasn't right for the movies?

CHARLES

I thought you looked lovely.

JESSICA

I felt—awful. (*Pause*) Jackie Mason seems like a nice boy.

CHARLES

He is.
    (*Pause.*)

JESSICA

Charley?

CHARLES

What?

JESSICA

Why are we so formal in here? Is it the room? We've suddenly become . . .
    (*She stops.*)

CHARLES

It must be the room, yes. You've suddenly become the mysterious and unattainable Jessica Lovell again.

JESSICA

I'm exactly the same Jessica Lovell I have been all along. No more mysterious and no more unattainable than before.

CHARLES

It must be me.

JESSICA

It must be. (*Suddenly he looks at her, their eyes meet.* JESSICA *senses something*) Oh! (*Suddenly* CHARLES *takes her into his arms and kisses her. He lets her go*) Your necktie's crooked, Charley. It's been such a late spring, hasn't it? You sure you wouldn't like some cold root beer? (*Suddenly* CHARLES *takes her into his arms again. This time her arms go around his neck and she returns his kiss warmly*) Oh, darling, darling . . .

CHARLES

I love you, Jessica . . .

JESSICA

Oh, yes, yes, I love you so much, Charley . . .

CHARLES

I've wanted to tell you . . .

JESSICA

I know—it's been awful—why didn't you?

CHARLES

I was scared . . .

JESSICA

So was I—scared you would—scared you wouldn't . . .
(*They kiss*) Oh, darling, what are we going to do?

CHARLES

I don't know—but right at this moment I don't care.

JESSICA

Everybody's going to find out.

CHARLES

I suppose so.
(*They kiss*.)

JESSICA

When did you first know, Charley?

CHARLES

That day you twisted your ankle.

JESSICA

I thought that was when.

CHARLES

I wanted to say something then . . .

JESSICA

I know. I thought you were going to.

CHARLES

I was scared.
(*They kiss*.)

JESSICA

Oh, Charley, if we had only . . .

CHARLES

Only what?

JESSICA

Nothing.

CHARLES
(*Thoughtfully*)
If we had only—met somewhere else, you mean, instead of in Clyde?

JESSICA

No, Charles!

CHARLES

So people would think that I . . .

JESSICA
(*Quickly*)
Do you think I care what people think?

CHARLES

I suppose if I lived here on Johnson Street—everything would be all right.

JESSICA

Don't *say* that, Charley!

CHARLES

And your father—he won't like it at all, will he?

JESSICA

He won't mind so much—honestly he won't—if he gets to know about it—gradually—and not all at once. (*She sees* CHARLES *frown and goes on hurriedly*) I mean—if he could just see something of you—for awhile—without knowing that . . .

CHARLES

That his daughter's in love with a boy from Spruce Street?

JESSICA

Charley! Nothing in the world matters but you! Nothing!
(*She clings to him.* CHARLEY *kisses her. After a moment
we hear:*)

LOVELL'S VOICE
(*Offstage*)

Jessica! Is that you?
(JESSICA *starts away, nervously.*)

JESSICA

Oh! Yes, Father.

LOVELL

Ah, good! We'll be right in.

JESSICA
(*Nervously*)

I thought he would be in bed.
(MR. LOVELL *and* MALCOLM BRYANT, *now about thirty-
four, enter.*)

LOVELL

And this is the wallpaper I was telling you about. (*To*
JESSICA) I didn't hear you come in. I saw the light and . . .
(*He sees* CHARLES) Oh! Well, well, I didn't know we had
company.

JESSICA

You know Charles Gray, don't you, Father?

LOVELL

Of course I know Charles Gray, Jessica—or *of* Charles
Gray. Where on earth did you find him? Not that I'm not
very glad that you *did* find him. (*He shakes hands with*
CHARLES) How do you do, Charles?

CHARLES

How do you do, sir?

LOVELL

Jessie, this is Mr. Malcolm Bryant. (*To* MALCOLM) My daughter, Jessica.

JESSICA

How do you do?

MALCOLM

I've been wanting to meet you, Miss Lovell. I've seen you around town a couple of times.

LOVELL

Mr. Bryant has just returned from studying the head hunters in Borneo and now he is making a social survey of Clyde.

JESSICA

I imagine you'll find some remarkable specimens in Clyde. This is Mr. Gray, Mr. Bryant.

MALCOLM

I'm glad to meet you, Mr. Gray. Do you live here in Clyde?

CHARLES

Yes, I live here. On Spruce Street.

LOVELL

That was not a happy remark of mine when I asked where Jessica found you. I'm delighted to have a Gray in the house.

MALCOLM

I'm still trying to orient myself. It's a little hard to get the general structure here, but, my God, it's a wonderful town —a beautiful, static, organized community. Let's see, your first name is Charles, isn't it?

CHARLES

That's right.

MALCOLM

Why don't we get on a first-name basis? I'm Malcolm, you're Charley, you're Jessie. Now let me get this straight. You're a college man, aren't you, Charley?

CHARLES

How did you know?

MALCOLM

Because it's my business to know social groups. Look at Jessica. She has Smith written all over her.

JESSICA

Vassar, please.

MALCOLM

Same pattern. Is your father a college man, Charley?

LOVELL

Charles' father was at Harvard with me for a short time— until he left us after Freshman midyears. Let's see, you went to Dartmouth, if I remember, Charles.

CHARLES

Yes, that's right, sir.

MALCOLM

Now why was that?

CHARLES

My aunt put me through college. She preferred Dartmouth

LOVELL

I was extremely sorry to hear about your Aunt Jane, Charles.

CHARLES

Thank you, sir.

MALCOLM

Why, what did she do?

CHARLES
(*Flatly*)

She died.

MALCOLM

Oh, I beg your pardon.

CHARLES

A few weeks ago.

LOVELL

Heart, wasn't it, Charles?

CHARLES

Yes, sir.

LOVELL

Yes, everyone has always known about the Grays. "The Gray Heart," we speak of. I'm very sorry. Well . . . (*He turns to* JESSICA) Mr. Bryant is very anxious to see the rest of the house. (*He turns to* CHARLES) So, Charles, in case I don't see you again I'll say good-bye. Give your father my regards. Turn out the lights when Charles goes, Jessica.

MALCOLM

Good-bye, Charley. I want to meet your father some time.

CHARLES

All right.

MALCOLM

My God, it's a wonderful town! (*To* MR. LOVELL *as they go*)
It's a way of life that has just the continuity I'm looking for.

LOVELL

My great-grandfather . . .
  (*Their voices fade out.*)

JESSICA

You know, Charley, I think he likes you.

CHARLES

I don't see why you think so.

JESSICA

Because he talked so much and . . .
  (*She hesitates.*)

CHARLES

—and I didn't do anything wrong . . .

JESSICA

Oh, Charley, don't! Father's not like that at all.

CHARLES

Never mind, Jessica. Everything's going to be all right.

JESSICA

Oh, it's got to, Charley! It's got to! I—I feel so terribly
lonely. It's awful—being an only child. Of course, I love
Father—but—well, he's always wanted me to be so perfect.
I suppose that's because Mother died suddenly when I was
only six—I never really belonged anywhere. I used to watch
the children go along Johnson Street to school—I had a gov-
erness, of course. I played with them a little but I never really
got to know them. And when I went away to school—Father
always brought me home week-ends. —Oh, dear, I sound like
Emily Dickinson, don't I?

CHARLES

No, Jessie.

JESSICA

It's just as though I'd been asleep, or almost asleep, until
that day I met you. I don't know what happened then. I don't
see why you liked me.
(*She looks at him earnestly.*)

CHARLES

I guess it was that red hat—and your hair. And you seemed
to be looking for someone and there wasn't anybody there
but me.
(*They kiss. We hear the voices of* MR. LOVELL *and* MAL-
COLM BRYANT, *returning.*)

LOVELL'S VOICE

Well, you see, my great-great-grandfather . . .

JESSICA

Oh, dear!

CHARLES

We've certainly got to break him of that habit.

LOVELL'S VOICE

. . . Ezra Lovell, built and improved the house on River
Street before the Revolutionary War. He was in the coastal
trade. (*They enter*) Why, Charles, still here? Fine! Jessie,
Mr. Bryant is leaving.

CHARLES

I'll be saying good night now, too.

MALCOLM

I'll walk along with you, if I may.

CHARLES

Certainly.

LOVELL
(*Extending his hand*)
Good night, Charles.

CHARLES

Good night, sir.

LOVELL

It was nice of you to entertain Jessica. I like to have her see young people. I'm afraid Jessica's altogether too inclined to stick to her home. Perhaps we'll see you some time again.

JESSICA
(*Laughing*)
Some time again? Charles has promised to take me to a movie again tomorrow night, haven't you, Charles?

CHARLES

Yes—yes . . .

LOVELL

Really, Jessica—two movies in a row . . .

JESSICA

Don't forget, Charles.
(*She looks at him archly.*)

CHARLES

I won't. Good night, Jessica.

JESSICA

Good night.

CHARLES

Good night, sir.

LOVELL

Good night, Charles.

MALCOLM

Good night, Mr. Lovell. Good night, Jessie.

LOVELL

Good night, Mr. Bryant.
(*The lights dim out. In the darkness we hear:*)

JESSICA

Oh, Father, isn't he very nice?

LOVELL

Yes, Jessica, but I wouldn't get too interested.
(*The lights come up on Johnson Street.* MALCOLM *and* CHARLES *come in.*)

MALCOLM

Of course he would have that attitude, Charley. Laurence Lovell is a typical dessicated stuffed shirt with an absurd approach to everything. Jessica is a perfect tribal type, except that there are very few virgins in primitive societies.

CHARLES

You seem to think you know a lot about people just by looking at them, don't you?

MALCOLM

That's my business. And another thing! Her father is in love with her, of course.

CHARLES

What the hell do you mean by that?

MALCOLM

Oh, that's not too uncommon in certain groups. Of course, basically, Jessica is equally in love with him. It's a standard pattern, as old as the first decadent civilization. Look at this street! You couldn't find a row of houses equal to that anywhere in the world, Charley. And all the Johnson Street people inside of them doing precisely the same thing at the given moment. My God, it's a wonderful town. Just how well do you know the Lovells, Charley?

CHARLES

What? Oh, not very well.

MALCOLM

You're not quite in the same group, are you?

CHARLES

No, why?

MALCOLM

Still it seemed to me you were great friends with Jessica.

CHARLES

Look, suppose you mind your own business.

MALCOLM

That's just the thing you *had* to say. I should have known it. Not sore, are you?

CHARLES

No, I guess not.

MALCOLM

You see, you interest me. Charley, you have the greatest happiness vouchsafed any human being.

CHARLES

How do you figure that out?

MALCOLM

Because you're an integrated, contented part of a group. You understand your taboos and rituals, you're working happily under an almost immobile system. But don't try to break out of your group, Charley . . .

CHARLES

Look, if I want to break out of my group I will.

MALCOLM

That's just the thing you *had* to say, Charley! Perfect! Not sore, are you?

CHARLES

Are you trying to tell me not to see Jessica Lovell?

MALCOLM

It's just this, Charley, the social tribal structure is the same all over the world. In general stay away from the chief class or the *alii,* as they call it in Polynesia—unless you happen to be in it. Don't try to marry the head man's daughter.

CHARLES

And just why not?

MALCOLM

You lose mobility. It isn't any fun. You get mixed up in new rituals you know nothing about—new taboos you aren't educated emotionally to follow. Now as it is, *you're* mobile. You can move either up or down. You see, we all fit into a pattern, Charley.

CHARLES

That's just what you *had* to say. Perfect.

MALCOLM

But Jessica—her pattern makes it impossible for her to move anywhere at all. She has to remain exactly where she is—because she's in the "upper-upper" stratum . . . (*He snaps his fingers*) There! That's the way I want to classify Clyde. There will be the three classes: the upper, the middle and the lower. Then I'll subdivide each one of these into the upper-upper, the middle-upper . . .

CHARLES

Here's where I turn off.

MALCOLM

Oh, Spruce Street down that way? Want to see it. Meet your family. From what I hear your father's hard to classify.

CHARLES

Some other time.

MALCOLM

Why?

CHARLES

It's a little late.

MALCOLM

You don't let anybody get away with anything, do you, Charley? You've got a tough mind.

CHARLES

Thanks. And Malcolm, I think you'll be surprised at what a democratic place Clyde really is.

MALCOLM

You do? Well, I hope you never find out different, Charley. And you won't—unless you try to break out of your class.

CHARLES

What do you think you need to break . . .

MALCOLM

Well, in Borneo, you have to have more shrunken heads . . .

CHARLES

And in Clyde?

MALCOLM

That's tougher. Here you need wampum—but it can't be just any wampum—it's got to mellow—it's got to be old wampum that your grandfather made or stole or however he got it. Still, wampum mellows faster now than it used to. Times change.

CHARLES
(To himself)

Wampum.

MALCOLM

That's right. Good night, Charley. My God! It's a wonderful town!

(MALCOLM *goes off. The lights fade to a single spotlight on* CHARLES. *Church bells are heard ringing in the distance. The lights come up on the* GRAYS' *living room.* JOHN GRAY *is seated at his desk.*)

JOHN GRAY

What's the matter, Charles? You look as though you were thinking.

CHARLES

Yes, I—was thinking of something I want to do.

(CHARLES *turns and moves into the living room as* JOHN GRAY *looks in the direction of the bells.*)

JOHN GRAY

That's the Baptist bell. Do you realize it's always behind the Congregationalist? Of course my experience is almost completely without validity, but I've found it's usually a great deal better to think of doing something than to do it. Now take this paper I'm writing for the confounded Sibley Club. It was much better thinking about it than doing it. Do you know how many tugboats there used to be in Clyde in the year 1902?

CHARLES

No.

JOHN GRAY

Well, there's not the slightest reason you should. But actually there used to be four tugboats tied up between the Nickerson Cordage Company and the old coal packet in 1902. Their names were the *Lizzie K. Simpkins,* named, I think, after the wife of Captain Simpkins who ran her, although he was living with another lady at the time . . . Am I boring you, Charles?

CHARLES

No—No . . .

JOHN GRAY

I suppose you have no interest in the river. When I was your age I was on it all the time in my catboat. I knew every rock in it.

CHARLES

I never had the chance. You were always going to buy me a boat and teach me to sail—but you never did.

JOHN GRAY

Why, that's true, I didn't. Why didn't you ask me more often?

CHARLES

I asked you and asked you, but you never got around to it. When we had the money you were too busy with that—and when we didn't . . .

JOHN GRAY

Well, well, that's very depressing. And I'm already rather depressed this evening—so perhaps you'd better go and let me finish this paper.

CHARLES

Father . . .

JOHN GRAY

Yes, Charles?

CHARLES

I want to make some money.
(*Pause.*)

JOHN GRAY
(*Regarding* CHARLES *carefully*)
Why, Charley, how very interesting.

CHARLES

I was thinking of getting a job in Boston. I don't believe I'm going to get anywhere if I stay at Wright-Sherwin, not for years and years.

JOHN GRAY

You couldn't be thinking of a brokerage office or a bond house, could you?

CHARLES

As a matter of fact—I was just thinking if you knew someone—if you wouldn't mind speaking to someone . . .

JOHN GRAY

Why, of course, Charles. I'd be delighted. This pleases me very much. It's about time you realized you can't get anywhere without money. It's strange so few people ever see it clearly.

CHARLES

I don't mean that money's everything.

JOHN GRAY

Oh, dear. Oh, dear me, of course it isn't. Naturally money isn't everything—but it seems to me that sometimes it helps.

CHARLES

I don't want anything for nothing. If I make money, I want to earn it.

JOHN GRAY

Yes, yes, of course you do—and that's very estimable. But do you remember what Jonathan Swift said about ambition?

CHARLES

I'm afraid not, Father.

JOHN GRAY

Oh, I wish you cared more for the polite adornments of the mind, Charles. He said: "Ambition often puts men upon doing the meanest offices: so climbing is performed in the same posture with *creeping*." I've never liked creeping.

CHARLES

And it would be creeping to want to get ahead?

JOHN GRAY

I think I can safely say that no one enjoys the comforts and pleasures to be derived from having money more than I—and yet I've never been able to creep for them. It has always been all or nothing with me. (*As* CHARLES *starts to speak, he holds up his hand*) Now, no lecture, please. I know you think *my* way of getting ahead was—unfortunate. But because of the handicaps of never having enough capital—I was unable to beat the system. The system is not fluid and it's very hard to beat.

CHARLES

What system?

JOHN GRAY

Why, the system under which we live. The order. There's always some sort of order. There's always the bundle of hay out ahead, for any ass who wants to get on, and They make it look like a very pleasant bundle.

CHARLES

Who are They?

JOHN GRAY

They are the people who own the hay. They are the people who run the system. And They have to toss out a little hay now and then to make the system work. They'll tell you there's plenty of hay for anyone who can get it. But the main thing is They don't want you to get it. It might be some of Their hay. You can get so far by effort, Charles. You will find that you can obtain a little hay but if you reach for more you'll get a sharp rap on the muzzle.

CHARLES

It seems to me that you've had a lot more hay than most people—at different times.

JOHN GRAY

Before I tried to get more of it, you mean? Now don't be so hard on me. I'm not going to do it again. That's all over.

CHARLES

What are you going to do with the seventy-five thousand dollars Aunt Jane left you?

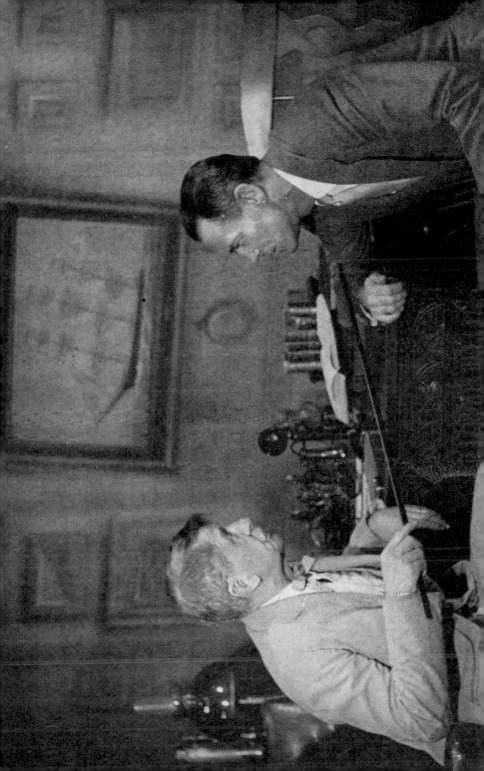

JOHN GRAY

How very blunt! I suppose I might ask you what you are
going to do with the five thousand dollars Aunt Jane left you,
but I won't.

CHARLES

I'm going to put it in government bonds. But are you going
to play the market with yours? I don't like to talk this
way . . .

JOHN GRAY

I know you don't. That's all right.

CHARLES

I don't care about myself—but what about Mother and
Dorothea? Why don't you set up a trust fund for them?

JOHN GRAY

An excellent idea. I'll have to think about it. Let's leave
it that way. You can watch me, and I'll think about it. (*He
stirs uneasily*) But however did we get switched onto me?
We were talking about you. How did this idea of your getting
a job in Boston ever get into your head?

CHARLES

Oh, it just came over me.

JOHN GRAY

It couldn't have anything to do with Jessica Lovell, could it?

CHARLES

How did you know?

JOHN GRAY

Oh, one pieces little things together—from here and there. I saw you together a few times—I met Jessica Lovell on the street and she seemed remarkably gracious to me—remarkably gracious!

CHARLES

Yes, it has something to do with Jessica Lovell.

JOHN GRAY

Are you in love with her?

CHARLES

Yes.
(*Pause.* JOHN GRAY *leans back.*)

JOHN GRAY

Well! Now, this really does me a lot of good. I wonder what Laurence Lovell will say. Did you see Laurence Lovell?

CHARLES

I met him tonight.

JOHN GRAY

I suppose you sat in the room with the wallpaper. Wasn't Laurence Lovell surprised to see you there?

CHARLES

He asked Jessica where on earth she found me.

JOHN GRAY

Oh, dear me.

CHARLES

But then he said it wasn't a happy remark.

JOHN GRAY

Oh, my. I never did like Laurence Lovell. You and I must certainly do something about this. We had better go up to Boston on Monday. (*He puts his hand on* CHARLES' *shoulder*) You really amaze me, Charles. There is a great deal to be said for love after all, isn't there? From now on you will want to do all the right things, wear the right clothes, meet the right people—all because you are in love with Jessica Lovell. Your life is changing . . . But remember, Charles, beware of too much ambition. Don't dull yourself to the refinements of life. Don't—creep—to your goal.

CHARLES

I won't, Father.

JOHN GRAY

That's good to know. (*The telephone rings and* JOHN GRAY *answers it*) Hello?

JESSICA'S VOICE

Mr. Gray, this is Jessica Lovell.

JOHN GRAY

Oh, good evening.

JESSICA'S VOICE

Is Charles there?

JOHN GRAY

Yes, he's right here, Jessica. Just hold on, please. (*He holds the phone out to* CHARLES) It's Jessica, Charles. (*As* CHARLES *takes the phone,* JOHN GRAY *leaves.*)

CHARLES
(*Into the phone*)
Hello.

JESSICA'S VOICE
Oh, darling, I had to call you before I went to sleep. I didn't have a chance to say good night to you properly.

CHARLES
(*Abruptly*)
Jessica, I'm going to get a job in Boston.
(*A moment's pause.*)

JESSICA'S VOICE
Why?

CHARLES
Because I love you. I want to make some money.

JESSICA'S VOICE
(*Worried*)
But if you go to Boston I won't see you.

CHARLES
Yes, you will. You can come down there to see me.

JESSICA'S VOICE
(*Suddenly excited*)
Oh, yes—yes, of course I can. I can come and stay with my aunt sometimes—we can have dinner—go to the theatre . . .

CHARLES

Even see each other in public without your father's knowing . . . (*A sudden pause*) What did he say after I left?

JESSICA'S VOICE
(*Faintly*)

Not to—get too interested in you. (*Suddenly frightened*)
Oh, Charley, he will like you! Give him time! Oh, I wish he
had sixteen children, all of them girls! Please don't be cross,
darling.

CHARLES

I'm not—I won't be. I'm so anxious to get started, Jessica.

JESSICA'S VOICE

Oh, yes, so am I!

CHARLES

I'll see you tomorrow night.

JESSICA'S VOICE

Yes—yes—good night, darling.

CHARLES

Good night, Jessica.
(*He hangs up. He thinks a moment and starts to pace
around the room.*)
Mr. Lovell—there's something I've been wanting to say to
you—about—er—er . . .
(*The lights fade to a single spotlight on him. Suddenly
his face takes on a determined expression.*)
Now I won't waste time beating around the bush. I'll come
straight to the point. Jessica and I are in love and we want

to get married. I naturally hope you're not going to have any objections but whether you like it or not . . .

(*He stops, shaking his head, hopelessly.*)

Mr. Lovell, I want to ask you for the hand of your daughter in marriage . . . Bah!

(*He grimaces in disgust.*)

Good evening, Mr. Lovell. Yes, it *is* a nice evening, isn't it? Yes, I did want to say something to you. You see, Jessica and I want to get married. (*He waits, anxiously. Suddenly his face lights up. He holds out his hand, shaking* MR. LOVELL's) Why, thank you, sir.—You've been expecting it, eh?— That's very kind of you, sir. (*He laughs*) Well, we told you just as soon as we . . . You see, sir, I wanted to make a little money before I . . . Oh, I know, money isn't everything, sir, but it seems to me sometimes it helps. And with a girl like Jessica . . . You see, my Aunt Jane left me five thousand dollars and . . . Yes, I did, I played the market. Oh, I was very careful and I'm out of it now for good. (*Modestly*) Well, it wasn't really clever of me, sir. I don't like the market. But I pyramided and I made about a hundred thousand dollars.

BLACKOUT

(*The lights come up on the wallpaper room. We see* JESSICA *and* MR. LOVELL *seated.* CHARLES *enters.*)

LOVELL

Good evening, Charles. Jessica tells me you want to see me about something.

CHARLES

Yes, sir.

LOVELL

Well, sit down. I hope nothing is wrong with your job in Boston?

CHARLES

No, sir. Everything's fine in Boston. I think I may even be in line for a promotion soon.

LOVELL

Well, that's fine, Charles. Your father's all right?

CHARLES

Oh, yes. Father's feeling very good these days.

LOVELL

I understand he's making a good deal in the market—on paper, that is.

CHARLES

Yes.

LOVELL

Well, you two got back early tonight. Didn't you go to the movies?

CHARLES

No, sir, we didn't. Not tonight.

JESSICA

We had dinner at the Shore Club.

LOVELL

The Shore Club? You're not a member, are you, Charles?

CHARLES

No, sir. My father is.

LOVELL

I didn't know that.

CHARLES

It's quite recent.

LOVELL

But how did you get there? I told you I didn't want you driving the Dodge at night, Jessica, and Charles hasn't a car, have you, Charles?

CHARLES

No, sir, but my father let me take his.

LOVELL

Oh, has your father a car? What kind is it?

CHARLES

A Cadillac.

LOVELL

Really. (*He sighs*) Well, perhaps you had better tell me what you wanted to say, Charles.

CHARLES

Mr. Lovell—I want to marry Jessica.
(*A pause.* MR. LOVELL *sits looking at him, stunned. There is a silence.*)

LOVELL

Pour me a glass of water, would you, please, Jessica?

CHARLES

You must have known, sir, that Jessica and I . . .

LOVELL

Yes, Charles. And I must apologize for my behavior. Believe me, this is no reflection on you at all.

CHARLES

I'm sorry you feel this way about it, sir, but I thought we ought to tell you.

LOVELL

Of course you had to tell me, Charles, but—oddly enough —for some reason—it never occurred to me that things had gone this far.

JESSICA

Father, we don't have to talk about it anymore now if . . .

LOVELL

Of course we do, Jessica. Now is just the time to talk about it. (*To* CHARLES) Well, Charles, you say you want to marry Jessica.

CHARLES

Yes, sir.

LOVELL

I take it that means you are in love with Jessica.

CHARLES

(*Smiling*)

Yes, sir. And I *do* know how you feel, sir. Jessica is used to a lot more than I'll be able to give her at the start, but—we are young and we do love each other.

LOVELL

How long have you known Jessica, Charles?

CHARLES

Why—all my life—I suppose . . .

LOVELL

No, I mean—how long have you been in love with Jessica?

JESSICA

Since this spring.

LOVELL

That's not very long, is it?

CHARLES

It's long enough to know that . . .

LOVELL

How old are you, Charles?

CHARLES

Twenty-five, sir.

LOVELL

Well, from all I hear you've done very well in Boston and I respect you for it. But as you point out, you will not be able to give Jessica everything she has been used to. And Jessica would never be quite the same in any other setting.

JESSICA

But Father, I don't care . . .

LOVELL

You would care, Jessica. Believe me you would. (*Again he turns to* CHARLES) How much are you earning in Boston? You don't mind my asking, do you?

CHARLES

No, sir. Sixty dollars a week.

LOVELL

Well, well, that's splendid. But, Charles! For a girl like Jessica . . .

JESSICA

But, Father, I tell you I don't care.

LOVELL

Jessica, you have no idea what this means. (*To* CHARLES) I don't wish to seem mercenary, but speaking realistically, Charles, it's hardly the time to talk about marrying Jessica now, is it?

CHARLES

Mr. Lovell, I have thirty-five thousand dollars besides that in government bonds.

(*A sharp pause.*)

LOVELL

Really! Did your father give it to you?

CHARLES

No, sir.

LOVELL

Did you make it yourself on the market?

CHARLES

Yes, sir. My Aunt Jane left me five thousand dollars and I . . .

LOVELL

I can't say I like that . . .

CHARLES

I don't either. But I wanted to marry Jessica. I didn't see any other way I could do it. I was desperate. If you knew how I felt about the market you would appreciate how desperate I was. And now that I do have the money, I see no reason . . .

LOVELL

You realize that money is one thing and stock-market money another.

CHARLES

I suppose so, but as long as you don't lose it, it's money.

LOVELL

Still it is not the same as inherited money.

CHARLES

Everyone has to start some time, doesn't he, sir? I suppose your family did once, Mr. Lovell. So unless you have some other reason, sir . . .

JESSICA

Father, we had to tell you, didn't we?

LOVELL

Jessica, please! In case neither of you knows it, marriage is a serious matter. When two people are infatuated . . .

CHARLES
(*Quietly*)
I don't think it's quite fair to call it that, sir.

LOVELL

Oh, yes, I realize that is a graceless word. But when two people are—well, first in love, let's say—it is quite impossible to know each other or to realize the complications of each other's backgrounds. Jessica is my only daughter and . . .

JESSICA

Oh, Father—Father . . .
(*A pause.* MR. LOVELL *seems suddenly tired.*)

LOVELL

Oh, very well. If things have gone this far, I suppose . . .
Very well, you may be engaged, but I don't want any public
announcement until we get to know each other better. I suppose you must tell your family, Charles, but no one else. I
want no engagement teas, no rounds of calling or other
jubilation until matters are more definitely resolved.

CHARLES

When do you think that would be, sir?

LOVELL
(*Sharply*)

We'll see, Charles.

CHARLES

What I want is to *marry* Jessica, sir. So the sooner we can
announce the engagement . . .

LOVELL
(*Sharper*)

There will be no announcement, Charles, until we are sure
we are ready.

CHARLES

Then it isn't really an engagement at all, is it?

JESSICA

Oh, Charley, please . . . We can be engaged—secretly—it
will be such fun.
(*A moment's pause.* CHARLES *looks at* MR. LOVELL.)

CHARLES

All right. Whatever you wish, sir.

LOVELL

That's—more reasonable, Charles. Well, I shall say good night.

CHARLES

I'm leaving now, sir.

LOVELL

Good night, Charles.

CHARLES

Good night, sir. And—thank you. (*He goes to* JESSICA) Good night, Jessica.

JESSICA

Good night. (*He kisses her.* MR. LOVELL *stands a moment, can't take it. He turns abruptly and goes out.* JESSICA *sees him and starts after him, hurt*) Father . . .

CHARLES

Jessica . . .

JESSICA

Oh, Charley, he's hurt . . .

CHARLES

Jessica, why can't you face it? It's going to hurt him *when*ever or *whom*ever you marry.

JESSICA

I just can't *bear* to see him hurt. Oh, Charley, if you could only just—well, just do what he says for a little while until . . . Just for now—until he gets more used to it.

(CHARLES *looks at her a moment.*)

CHARLES

All right, if that's the way you want it . . .

JESSICA

Oh, Charley . . .

(*She goes into his arms.*)

BLACKOUT

(*In the darkness the telephone is heard ringing, and after a moment the lights go up on the telephone at right. NANCY enters.*)

NANCY

Hello—Hello . . .

OPERATOR'S VOICE

Is this Sycamore Park 827?

NANCY

(*Quickly worried*)

Yes—yes—who's calling?

OPERATOR'S VOICE
I have a call for Mrs. Charles Gray.

NANCY
This is Mrs. Charles Gray. Who's calling, Operator?

OPERATOR'S VOICE
All right, sir, here's your party. Booth two, please, sir.
(*The lights go up on the telephone at left.* CHARLES *enters and picks up the phone. He is excited.*)

CHARLES
Hello—hello—Nancy?

NANCY
(*Sharply, worried*)
Charley—what's the matter?

CHARLES
Look, Nancy . . .

NANCY
Are you all right? What's happened?

CHARLES
Nothing—nothing . . .

NANCY
Charley, tell me. I can't bear it.

CHARLES

You were right, Nancy. She did do something to me way
back there.

NANCY

What? Who? Who did what?

CHARLES

Jessica Lovell. That's where it all started. I haven't thought
it all through yet but, my God, that's where it all started . . .

NANCY

Oh, I thought . . . Charley, have you been drinking?

CHARLES

Drinking? No. Why? Did I sound excited?

NANCY

Yes . . .

CHARLES

Oh, I guess I was a little. Were you asleep?

NANCY

Yes . . .

CHARLES

I'm sorry, Nance . . .

NANCY

That's all right. I got a little confused. What did you say about Jessica Lovell? Have you seen her?

CHARLES

No, I haven't seen her.

NANCY

You can if you want to.

CHARLES

I know I can if I want to but . . . Skip it, Nancy. I'll tell you when I get home. How are you, Nance?

NANCY

Well, I've been bearing up pretty well until now. What have you been doing?

CHARLES

Oh, nothing much. I registered at the hotel and it was too late to see anyone so I've been wandering around the streets looking at the houses. Our old house on Spruce Street looks a lot smaller than I remembered it. And it's been painted brown now. My father always had it white. (*He pauses a moment*) There're too many ghosts up here, Nancy.

NANCY

I told you there would be. Well, stop thinking now and go to bed. When are you coming home?

CHARLES

Just as soon as I can. Tomorrow I hope.

NANCY

Wonderful. If you don't come until Friday be sure to get home early, though. The Burtons, remember.

CHARLES

I know. How are the children?

NANCY

Well, there's no perceptible change.

CHARLES

What's happened since I left?

NANCY

Well, Bill cut his lip. A baseball hit him. And that man to wax the dining-room floor . . .

CHARLES

Yes?

NANCY

He never came.

CHARLES

Well, never mind. How about the Buick?

NANCY

What do you want to know about the Buick?

CHARLES

I don't know. I was just suddenly feeling lonely for you and the Buick.

NANCY

That's a nice association of ideas. The Buick's fine. It's asleep. How lonely are you?

CHARLES

Very lonely. I wish you were here.

NANCY

I'm glad you do. Come home as soon as you can and don't worry any more tonight about anything.

OPERATOR'S VOICE

Your three minutes are up . . .

NANCY
(*Hurriedly*)

All right, all right, we're all through, Operator. Don't put any more money in, Charley. Good night, darling . . .

CHARLES

Good night, Nance . . .

NANCY

I love you . . .

BLACKOUT

(*The lights go up on the* GRAYS' *living room.* JOHN GRAY, *looking very opulent, is standing talking to his wife while a tailor measures him.*)

TAILOR

(*Measuring his raised arm*)
Thirty-four and a quarter . . .
(*He jots the measurement down.*)

JOHN GRAY

—and eventually we could have a house in Pinehurst or Sea Island or Aiken. Oh, I have several plans in mind for us.

TAILOR

(*As he collects his materials from the couch*)
Thank you very much, Mr. Gray.

JOHN GRAY

I hope you make your train all right.

TAILOR

They'll all be ready for a try-on in two weeks' time. Good night. Good night, Mrs. Gray.

ESTHER

Good night.
(*The* TAILOR *exits as* CHARLES *enters.*)

JOHN GRAY

Ah . . .

ESTHER

Hello, Charley. Did you have a pleasant evening?

CHARLES

Yes, thank you, Mother.
(*He hesitates a moment, uncomfortably.*)

JOHN GRAY
(*Looking at him*)
What's happened to you, Charles?

CHARLES

Well, I might as well tell you. I'm engaged to Jessica, but I'm only to tell you and you're to tell no one. It isn't to be announced yet.

JOHN GRAY

Well . . .
(*He reaches for his coat.*)

ESTHER
(*Springing to her feet and kissing him*)
Oh, darling, I'm so happy. Of course, we knew you were attentive to Jessica but . . .

JOHN GRAY
(*When he has his coat on*)
Congratulations, Charles. I'm extremely happy for you.

CHARLES

Thank you.

ESTHER

Oh, Charley, isn't it wonderful!

CHARLES

Yes, yes, quite wonderful, Mother.

ESTHER

Well, I just think it's too exciting for words.

JOHN GRAY

I like Jessica Lovell very much. Did you—er—talk to Laurence Lovell?

CHARLES

Yes.

JOHN GRAY

Oh, my! I wish I had been there.

ESTHER

What did he say when you told him, Charles?

CHARLES

I don't think he liked it very much. He asked for a glass of water.

JOHN GRAY

Oh, dear me, a glass of water.

CHARLES

He said there should be no jubilation.

JOHN GRAY

Oh, my!

CHARLES

I don't think he thought it was serious until we began to talk about money.

JOHN GRAY

Why did he think it was serious then? I can't quite see that the salary you make would cause too deep an impression on Laurence Lovell.

CHARLES
(*Uncomfortably*)

Well—I have a few government bonds.

JOHN GRAY
(*Looking at him*)

Well— How much?

CHARLES
(*Reluctantly*)

Thirty-five thousand dollars.
(*A dead silence.* JOHN GRAY *sits up and looks at him, a small smile on his face.*)

ESTHER

Why, darling, how perfectly wonderful! Why didn't you ever tell us?

CHARLES

Well, no use discussing those things . . .

ESTHER

But I think it's perfectly—don't you, John?

JOHN GRAY
(*Who has been watching* CHARLES)

I do, indeed, Esther dear—it's perfectly. (*He looks at* CHARLES) Charles?

CHARLES
(*Guiltily*)

Yes, sir?

JOHN GRAY

It can't be—no, no, I'm sure not but—it can't be that you have—(*He whispers*)—played the market, Charles.

CHARLES

Well, I did for a little while.

JOHN GRAY

Oh, my!

CHARLES

I don't believe in it, you know.

JOHN GRAY

Naturally, naturally, I know you don't, Charles.

CHARLES

And I'm out of it for good.

JOHN GRAY

Of course. Well, well, I can only repeat: "The power of love is incalculable." But— (*He looks at* CHARLES) from what you say, I have the feeling that Laurence Lovell was mildly insulting.

CHARLES

I told you he didn't like it.

JOHN GRAY

And that's one part of it *I* don't like. I think I'd better go and see Laurence Lovell tomorrow.

CHARLES

No, Father.

JOHN GRAY

Yes, I think I will. What reason did he give for not telling anyone about the engagement?

CHARLES

He wants to wait until we know each other better.

JOHN GRAY

And you—agreed?

CHARLES

What else could I do?

JOHN GRAY

Oh, nothing—nothing—I presume . . .

CHARLES

I suppose you'd say I compromised . . .

JOHN GRAY

Oh, no—no . . .

ESTHER

Well, of course he didn't. And I think it would be very nice if we asked Mr. Lovell here to dinner. Don't you, John?

JOHN GRAY

No, Esther, I don't think it's necessary to go that far.

ESTHER

Well, I must tell Dorothea. She's gone to bed.

CHARLES

I wish you wouldn't tell . . . We're not supposed to tell anyone . . .

ESTHER

You've got to tell your own sister, Charles.

CHARLES

I'm afraid she'll spread it all over town.

ESTHER

I'll tell her not to tell. Oh, I'm so happy for you, Charley.
Engaged!
(*She goes out.*)
(CHARLES *stands there motionless.* JOHN GRAY *looks up
at him.*)

JOHN GRAY

For one who has just made such an important step toward
happiness, you are looking rather tired, Charles.

CHARLES

Yes, I am rather.

JOHN GRAY

I wouldn't work too hard. It doesn't pay. You can't beat the
system that way.

CHARLES

You can't beat it your way either. I hope you're being
careful.

JOHN GRAY

As careful as a banker, Charles. I'm as sound as Electric
Bond and Share. Shall I tell you something? I always wonder
why I am doing so well until I remember this is the first time
I've had any real working capital. You see, I'm pretty well
up in the system now. Just between you and me—don't tell

the ladies, it will only make them nervous—as of today—October 6, 1929—there is in the kitty six hundred and fifty thousand dollars.

CHARLES
(*Nervously*)
I don't like being out at sea in a canoe with just one paddle. When will you have enough, Father?

JOHN GRAY
Now are you going to lecture me again, Charles?

CHARLES
I know you're making a lot of money on paper, but why don't you get some of it off paper? I really wish you would, Father. The market is completely wild this year. The price of common stock has already discounted all conceivable earnings in any future time that you can see. It may still go up but it's terribly dangerous. At least take some of it and set up a trust fund for Mother and Dorothea.

JOHN GRAY
You may make a good investment man some day. That's very sound judgment. I'm going to do it—very soon. Now stop worrying and listen to an idea I have. Your mother and sister need a change. I was thinking of taking them on a trip. The Riviera—Monte Carlo . . . Even though I don't gamble myself, I've always wanted to watch those improvidents at Monte Carlo. Then Egypt, up the Nile, through to India, Japan, China . . . (*He looks at* CHARLES, *suddenly*) You're afraid of money, Charles.

CHARLES
(*Sincerely*)

Yes. I am.

JOHN GRAY

Well, I'm going to relieve your mind. I've been thinking over all you've said and I think you're right. You can carry a good thing too far, can't you? You know, I think I really ought to set a limit. I'm going to stop all this and cash in as soon as I've made a million.

BLACKOUT

(*A single light goes up on the* GRAYS' *living room.* JOHN GRAY *lies motionless, stretched out on the sofa, one leg and arm hanging down. On the floor is a newspaper, an empty glass and a pill bottle.* CHARLES *is kneeling, dazed. He places the limp arm upon the body, kisses the forehead, reaches for the bottle and rises. Slowly he places the bottle into his pocket. The lights fade and we hear slow bells tolling.*)

(*The lights go up on Johnson Street as the bells fade out.* MALCOLM BRYANT *enters, and in a moment* CHARLES *enters from the opposite side. He is very thoughtful, preoccupied.*)

MALCOLM

Hello, Charley.

CHARLES

Oh, hello, Malcolm.

MALCOLM

Can't tell you how sorry I am. I liked your father.

CHARLES

Yes—everybody always liked Father.

MALCOLM

What are you going to do, Charley?

CHARLES

Well, right at this moment I'm on my way to . . . Mr. Lovell sent for me.

MALCOLM

Sent for you? What do you mean "sent for you"? What's up, Charley?

CHARLES

I don't know. He wants to have a little talk with me. About wampum, maybe, or lack of it.

MALCOLM

When I was in Papua I lived in a nice clear tribe. There was a nice young fellow there—warrior class, not chief class . . . He fell in love with the Chief's third daughter. They made him produce six pigs and a canoe for the marriage rites. Then they made him wear the double nose ring and they tatooed the omoo bird insignia on his right buttock. You don't get those tatoos off when once they're on. Poor fella. He was out of his group. He was very unhappy. He began to lose weight right away. He wasn't mobile.

CHARLES

Okay, Malcolm. I get it.

MALCOLM

Look, Charley, I'm getting out tomorrow—my work's finished here—going to New York for a week—then I'm off to Afghanistan. Come along with me.

CHARLES

Before I get the omoo bird tatooed on my right buttock?

MALCOLM

You've been in Clyde long enough. Get some fresh air in your lungs.

CHARLES
(*Amused*)

From Clyde to Afghanistan in one step, eh?

MALCOLM

Sure.

CHARLES

Good Lord, Malcolm, I've got a job in Boston.

MALCOLM

You'd have a job with me. There's nothing more for you to get out of Clyde—and there's nothing more for you to get out of Boston either . . .

CHARLES

I've just got to get my whole life out of it, is all. Look, Malcolm, I'm doing pretty well in Boston. Even with things as they are, I've still got my job and Jessica and I . . . (*He hesitates and holds out his hand*) Well, so long, Malcolm.

MALCOLM

So long, Charley. Hope we run into each other again sometime.

CHARLES

I hope so too. Keep mobile.

MALCOLM

Same to you, Charley. So long.
(*He nods and starts off.* CHARLES *continues on his way.*)
(*The lights fade on Johnson Street and come up on the* LOVELLS' *wallpaper room as* CHARLES *enters.*)

LOVELL

Good evening, Charles. Thank you for coming over.

CHARLES

Good evening, sir. Is Jessica . . .

LOVELL

She's in the library. I haven't had the opportunity to tell you how sorry I am.

CHARLES

Thank you.

LOVELL

I have heard what you have done toward settling your father's affairs. I understand there was practically nothing left and you have put all your savings in trust for your mother and sister.

CHARLES

I prefer they don't know that—but think it's my father's estate.

LOVELL

Naturally. Now, Charles, nothing I have to say reflects on you personally, believe me. But there has been a change, and an unavoidable one, in the whole situation, and I am not referring to its financial aspects. Now I don't say there's anything verging on real scandal, Charles, but we must all face the implications of your father's sudden death at this especial time . . .

CHARLES

My father died of heart failure brought on by the strain of these last few days.

LOVELL

I know, Charles. But there is a doubt in people's minds. There always will be. Now I've thought this over carefully. I've been over it thoroughly with Jessica.

CHARLES

I'd like to see Jessica, please.

LOVELL

Jessica and I have been most unhappy. Most unhappy, I assure you. But it's an impossible situation, Charles. The whole thing is too impossible. We must end it. I hope you understand this, Charles.

CHARLES

I do. You have never thought I was good enough—or that I had enough money for Jessica.

LOVELL

That is very blunt, Charles.

CHARLES

I'd like to see Jessica, sir.

LOVELL

Very well. (*He walks over and calls*) Jessica, will you come in, please? (*He turns back into the room*) It's only fair that she should tell you herself. Fair for both of us.

(JESSICA *enters. She has been crying.*)

JESSICA

Oh, Charley—Charley . . .

LOVELL

Don't cry, Jessica, dear.

JESSICA

Oh, Charley, I'm so ashamed. I'm not fit to marry anyone.

LOVELL

Just tell Charles and then it will be all over, Jessie.

JESSICA

(*Sobbing*)

Oh, Charley, I can't marry you with both of you feeling the way you do—He's given up everything for me—I have to do what he thinks is best—Can't you see I'm all he has?

LOVELL

There, Jessica, it's all over now.

JESSICA

It doesn't mean I don't love you. I do. I do.

CHARLES

Then that's all there is to it, isn't it? Jessica, do you remember what you said one night? If I saw you getting away you wanted me to tell you?

JESSICA

(*Sobbing*)

Oh, Charley, don't—don't—I can't bear it any more . . . I can't—I can't—please don't make it harder . . .

CHARLES

You wanted me to tell you . . .

(JESSICA *turns away from him, sobbing. Slowly* CHARLES *straightens up. He is dazed. He turns and hurries from the room. The lights begin to fade.*)

JESSICA

Charley! Charley!

BLACKOUT

(In the darkness we hear:)

CONDUCTOR'S VOICE

Boston train! Train to Boston! Coaches in the rear! Smoking car ahead! Train for Boston! 'Board!

(We hear the noise of the train pulling out of the station. The lights come up on the day coach, CHARLES *sitting by one of the windows.* JACKIE MASON *and a* STRANGER *enter.* JACKIE *halts by* CHARLES.*)*

JACKIE
(To the STRANGER*)*

See you in the smoker. *(To* CHARLES*)* Here you are. Been looking all through the train for you.

CHARLES

Oh, hello, Jackie.

JACKIE

Well, how'd things go? Find out all you wanted to know?

CHARLES
(Abruptly)

What?

JACKIE

About the Nickerson Cordage Company.

CHARLES

Oh! Yes, I did.

JACKIE

Good. Well, how did it seem coming back to the old place?

CHARLES

Sort of nice, Jackie.

JACKIE

Pretty little town.

CHARLES

Yes. It hadn't changed as much as I thought it would.

JACKIE

Nothing changes very much in Clyde.

CHARLES

I wandered around—saw some of the old landmarks . . .
    (*A moment's pause.*)

JACKIE

I'm sorry you didn't get to see Jessica.

CHARLES

I just couldn't make it, Jackie.

JACKIE

She knew you were here. (*Slight pause*) You see, there's
something I was going to tell you—on the train yesterday
but—I hope you'll understand, Charley.

CHARLES
    (*Looking at him*)

Understand what?

JACKIE

Well, you see—I've been seeing a lot of Jessica. (*He laughs,
deprecatingly*) I guess Mr. Lovell thought I was pretty harm-
less, but things can't help changing and that's what I wanted
to tell you. I want to tell you that Jessica and I are engaged
and are going to be married in June.
    (*A sudden pause.* CHARLES *looks at him, dumbfounded.*)

CHARLES

Well!

JACKIE

Yes. You see, for years we didn't do anything but talk about you—and then—one day—well, as I say, things change.

CHARLES

How did—Mr. Lovell take it?

JACKIE

Well, I was a little surprised. He didn't seem to mind. It's funny when I had my talk with him he kept calling me Charles. Of course his mind isn't what it used to be. But he's really a grand old gentleman—and we'll all be living there together.

CHARLES

You're going to live there—with them?

JACKIE

Oh, yes, of course. He couldn't live without Jessica. As a matter of fact, I don't know if she could without him. They're very devoted. Really touching to see something as fine as that in this day and age.

(CHARLES *suddenly draws a deep breath. A little shudder passes over him which he shakes off. He turns to* JACKIE *sincerely.*)

CHARLES

(*Sincerely*)

I think it's splendid, Jackie. I wish you and Jessica all the happiness in the world.

JACKIE

Thanks, Charley, thanks a lot.
(*A moment's pause.*)

CHARLES

So you're going to be married in June?

JACKIE

That's right. Although this is all confidential, Charley.
We're not going to announce it right away.
(*A sudden pause.* CHARLES *stares at him.*)

CHARLES

You're not?

JACKIE

No—we're keeping it a secret for awhile.

CHARLES

Did Mr. Lovell ask for a glass of water?

JACKIE

Why, yes, as a matter of fact, he did.

CHARLES

Did he say anything about there being no—jubilation?

JACKIE

Why, yes, he used that very word. How did you know?
(CHARLES *leans forward, earnestly, sincerely.*)

CHARLES

Listen, Jackie! You and Jessica get married in June! Don't
let anything stop you, will you?

JACKIE

No, Charley.

CHARLES

You won't mind living there on Johnson Street with them, will you?

JACKIE

No, I think it will be fine.

CHARLES

So do I. Don't let anything stop you.

JACKIE

No.

(CHARLES *suddenly becomes very happy.*)

CHARLES
(*Elated*)

Well, I think that's fine. Fine? Hell! I think it's wonderful! Listen, Jackie, we always used to stick together, didn't we?

JACKIE

We sure did, Charley.

CHARLES

Well, we're still sticking together. Look, Jackie, let's celebrate—you and me.

JACKIE

Okay.

CHARLES

When we get to Boston let's you and me take the town apart.

JACKIE

My God, if you don't sound like the old Charley Gray.

CHARLES

I *am*, Jackie. (*He slaps him on the knee*) My God, it's good to see you, Jackie.

JACKIE

Wonderful to see you, Charley.

CHARLES

You haven't changed a bit.

JACKIE

You're the same old Charley Gray.

CHARLES
(*Slapping his knee again*)

Jackie Mason . . .

JACKIE

Charley Gray . . .

Curtain

ACT THREE

ACT THREE

The same as Act One, Scene I. The GRAYS' *living room. Early evening.*

As the curtain rises, CHARLES *and* NANCY *are seated having cocktails with* MR. *and* MRS. BURTON. *The women are in long dresses; the men are in dinner coats, the only difference being that* CHARLES *is wearing a soft shirt and* MR. BURTON *a stiff one.* CHARLES *is bored and restless.*

BURTON

You know, everything—*everything* fits into banking somewhere. Essentially, banking is only knowing how to use extraneous knowledge. It is the oldest and the most basically human business there is in the world. In fact, I don't even like to think of banking as a business or even as a profession. It may startle you a little to hear me say this, but I'm very sure I'm right—banking, for a good banker, is an art. Don't you agree with me, Charles?

CHARLES
(Uneasily)

Well, it depends on . . .

NANCY
(Quickly)

I see your point, Mr. Burton. It's very well taken.

MRS. BURTON

What were you going to say it depends on, Mr. Gray?

155

CHARLES

Well, I suppose it depends on your definition of art.

BURTON
(*Looking at him, coolly*)

You know, sometimes you have a very cryptic quality, Charley. I never seem to know lately whether you're laughing at me or not. Sometimes you're an enigma.

CHARLES
(*Smiling*)

Well, you're not exactly an open book yourself, Tony.

MRS. BURTON

It's a good thing for Tony to have someone an enigma. Everybody licks Tony's boots so. That's why he's so impossible when he comes home. (*To* NANCY) Is Mr. Gray impossible when he comes home, my dear?

NANCY
(*Glaring at* CHARLES)

Impossible!

MRS. BURTON

I wonder what they do at the bank. Especially before nine and after three. I have a few vague ideas. That blonde secretary of Tony's . . .

NANCY

Not before nine, certainly.

MRS. BURTON

We'll compare notes after dinner.

BURTON

Even if it isn't *exactly* an art, Charley, you must agree that all experiences of any kind can be used in banking. For example, you remember that Mrs. Burton and I took a little trip in 1933. You hadn't been with us long then. Things were pretty tense in 1933, so we decided to go away. We went to Bagdad.

CHARLES

Why Bagdad?

NANCY
(*Quickly*)

It must be a fascinating place!

BURTON

It was. You really should go there some time, Nancy.

NANCY

I'd like nothing better.

BURTON

The cruise ship stopped at Beirut and from there Mrs. Burton and I took the side trip. We went on a bus that was, incredibly enough, as comfortable as a Greyhound bus right here in America.

(*The telephone rings long and loud in the next room. Both* MR. *and* MRS. BURTON *jump up, excitedly. They speak simultaneously.*)

MRS. BURTON

That must be our call to Barbara . . .

BURTON

There's Barbara at last . . .
    (*They both start out, then stop and look at* NANCY, *awkwardly.*)

MRS. BURTON

Oh, I beg your pardon . . .

BURTON

Sorry . . .

NANCY

No, no, go right ahead. It's always long distance when it
rings like that.

MRS. BURTON

It's just that we tried an hour to get Barbara before we left
home . . .

NANCY

Please! Go right ahead.
    (MRS. BURTON *exits.*)

CHARLES

We won't be a minute—at least *I* won't! When Mrs. Burton
gets on the phone with her daughter . . .

NANCY

It's perfectly all right.

(MR. BURTON *exits.* NANCY *turns back into the room and faces* CHARLES. CHARLES *looks at her.*)

CHARLES

All right, don't say it!

NANCY

But why do you have to disagree with *everything* he says? "It depends on your definition of art." "You're not exactly an open book yourself, Tony." "Why Bagdad?" At least let the man open his mouth without . . . And you wore a soft shirt after all instead of the stiff one I laid out for you!

CHARLES

I'm not going to wear a stiff shirt just because Tony Burton does!

NANCY

Oh, I hate it when you act this way! It's all because you went up there to Clyde! You've acted differently ever since you came back.

CHARLES

Maybe I have. I had a lot of time to think. (*He turns away*) Oh, it's all so damned contrived!

NANCY

What is?

CHARLES

All of it! So superficial! The bank president and the big job, and what will happen to Junior—will he get to Exeter —and whether a boiled shirt will help. The values of it are childish. It hasn't any values at all!

NANCY

But you want the job . . .

CHARLES

Nancy, don't be so tense. Maybe it isn't as important as all that. Anyway . . .

NANCY

Don't say it! I can't stand it if you say it!

CHARLES

What do you think I'm going to say?

NANCY

That we have each other! I *know* we have each other but I don't want to hear it! It's been in your mind ever since you came home. Tell me later but don't tell me now!

CHARLES

Nancy, I'm doing everything I can . . .

NANCY

You're not! You're acting licked already.

CHARLES

Maybe I don't give a damn.

NANCY

And now I suppose you're going to say I've always been pushing you.

CHARLES

I wish you'd stop telling me what I'm going to say.

NANCY
(*Turning away, upset*)

Oh, it's not fair, it's not fair!
(*Suddenly they hear the* BURTONS *offstage.* NANCY *turns quickly and recovers.*)

MRS. BURTON
(*Offstage*)

I think Miss Smith is the red-headed one. Barbara likes her.

CHARLES

What isn't?

BURTON
(*Offstage*)

I really think we're going to have some luck this time, Althea.

MRS. BURTON

Oh, I do hope so.

NANCY

Here they come— (CHARLES *has gone to the cocktail shaker*) Charley, you're not going to have another cocktail?

CHARLES
(*Gloomily*)

Maybe I am and maybe I'm not.
(*The* BURTONS *enter.* NANCY *goes to them with a smile.*)

NANCY

Well, I take it, it was Barbara.

MRS. BURTON

No, it wasn't. It was one of the teachers. Barbara had gone down to the village but they expect her back any minute. I told her to have Barbara call us here, if you're sure it's all right.

CHARLES

Oh, perfectly. Isn't it, Nancy?

NANCY

Of course—although it frightens me.

CHARLES

It does me, too.

MRS. BURTON

What does?

CHARLES

Why—the same thing that frightens Nancy.

NANCY

(*Quickly*)

To think of the time when Evelyn will have to go away to school.

CHARLES

Yes, that's it.

NANCY

I don't know what we'd do without her.

CHARLES

Certainly don't.

MRS. BURTON

I know, I felt the same way, too.

BURTON

Having another cocktail, Charles?

(NANCY *looks over, quickly.*)

CHARLES

I was just debating.

BURTON

Oh, come on. Won't hurt us to relax a bit and tomorrow's Saturday.

(NANCY *looks relieved.*)

CHARLES

Good.

(*He pours the cocktails.*)

BURTON

Well, we spent the night in quite a nice French hotel in Damascus, where Mrs. Burton bought that rare rug we have now in the library. My, it was hot! Remember, Althea?

MRS. BURTON

Yes, it was hot.

BURTON

There was plenty of ice water, though. Then at dawn we started right across the desert and toward the next evening the bus stopped at a place called Rutba Wells, right out in the middle of nowhere. Fortunately, it was run by the British and so was sanitary. And then, in the cool of the evening we went right across the desert to Bagdad—and there it was at dawn . . .

MRS. BURTON
(*To* NANCY)

It really was romantic.

NANCY

It must have been.

BURTON

A city on a muddy river, spanned by a bridge of boats. The next morning we went to the museum to see the ancient treasures from—er . . .

MRS. BURTON

Ur.

BURTON

Ur—Ur. And we met a man there—and this is the most exciting part—and he showed us some mud bricks that were actually parts of an account book. When you got used to them, you could see how they balanced their figures; and on one brick, believe it or not, there was even an error in addition that had been preserved through the centuries. Now what do you think of that, Charley?

CHARLES

Well—I'd say that . . .

NANCY
(*Quickly*)

It's incredible.

BURTON

Yes, it was. Yes, that meant a great deal to me. Well . . . (*He raises his glass to* NANCY *and they drink*) Nancy, my dear, I wish you wouldn't always surprise me so.

NANCY

What have I done now?

BURTON

It seems to me you are so much more beautiful every time I see you. Or do I just forget?

NANCY

It might be that you just forget, mightn't it?

BURTON

We've really got to do something about seeing each other more often. Why don't you come to work some morning instead of Charles? I'm getting pretty sick of seeing Charley around.

(NANCY *catches her breath.*)

CHARLES

(*Smiling*)

Perhaps I'd better start looking for a job somewhere else.

BURTON

(*After a moment, puzzled*)

You know, Charles, I wish there weren't so many words, or it may be because I'm getting old that they confuse me more than they used to. Somehow they keep having more shades of meaning. Now even with Charles and me it's difficult. I say a word and he says a word and we can look it up in the dictionary, but it doesn't mean the same thing to either of us and it would mean something a little different to you, Nancy, and it would be something a little different to Althea. I don't suppose this is a very new thought of mine, but it's a thought.

MRS. BURTON

I'm not even sure it's a thought. Tony, I haven't the faintest idea of what you're talking about.

BURTON

But Charley knows, don't you, Charley? We both may be worrying about the same thing but we worry about it in different ways.

CHARLES

(*Slowly*)

Yes, I think I know what you mean. If we are both worried about the same thing—naturally your worry approaches it from one angle—and mine from quite a different one.

(NANCY *looks frightened.*)

BURTON

Exactly. I wish we could all get together, we might do something with the world, but of course we never can get together. That's the exasperating part of it.

MRS. BURTON

Really, Tony, I think you've had enough of that cocktail. (*To* NANCY) Have you the slightest dea of what he's getting at?

NANCY

I'm not sure.

BURTON

Perhaps *I'm* being cryptic now, but all I'm saying is that I wish we might all be friends. I really hope we can be, no matter what may happen in the future, and the future isn't as clear as it used to be. That's all I'm trying to say. I just want us all to be friends, no matter what happens.

(*A moment's pause.* NANCY *is stricken,* CHARLES *turns away for a moment, then back.* TONY *is looking at* CHARLES.)

CHARLES
(*Casually*)
Why, of course, we'll all be friends, Tony.

BURTON
Fine. That's fine!
(*Again the telephone rings loud and long. Again the*
BURTONS *jump up but this time* MR. BURTON, *being nearer
the door, gets a head start.*)

MRS. BURTON
Now that *must* be Barbara!

BURTON
(*On his way out*)
You don't mind?

NANCY
No, no, of course not.
(MR. BURTON *exits.*)

MRS. BURTON
We'll try to make it short. Of course, when Mr. Burton and
Barbara get to talking . . .
(*She exits. A pause.* CHARLES *takes a deep breath.*)

CHARLES
Well, I guess that's that. I'm sorry, Nance. I had the feeling
it was coming.

NANCY

Oh, my God, my God, I didn't! I thought sure you were going to get it!

(*She cries softly.*)

CHARLES

He's been too nice all evening. He was trying to give me something soft to fall on.

NANCY

Oh, Charley, what are we going to do?

CHARLES

I don't know. These things are always awkward. It's embarrassing for Tony, too. Perhaps I'd better resign. (NANCY *wilts;* CHARLES *sits, depressed*) I think when Tony said that about always being friends—that's what he meant. I suppose he can get me in somewhere else. Although I'll probably never have as good a position as the one I have now.

NANCY

(*With a sob*)

Oh, God! After all these years!

CHARLES

We might as well face it. In a business way I've gone as far as I will go. (*He gives a wry smile*) You know what really shocks me most?

NANCY

What?

CHARLES

I thought I had myself all prepared for any bad news I might get—that I wouldn't think it was complete disaster if I got it—but now—(*He puts his hand to his stomach*)—right here—in the pit of my stomach . . .

NANCY

Mine, too.
    (*A moment's pause.* CHARLES *takes a deep breath.*)

CHARLES

Well, anyway, thank God it's over. Stomach or no stomach —I feel as if I can take a deep breath again. There's nothing more to expect from Tony Burton. If I want to say "Why Bagdad?" to him, from now on, I can.

NANCY

You said it anyway.

CHARLES

Yes—but now I can say it without being afraid. Or, what's even more important, now I don't even *have* to say it. (*They sit a moment in silence.* CHARLES *is very thoughtful*) We can sell this house and move into a smaller one. We won't starve —after all, I can make . . . (NANCY's *head sinks into her hands*) We'll get enough to educate Bill and Evvie. We'll never make the Hawthorn Hill Club now, of course—but who cares? I never really wanted to be in that club anyway.

NANCY

I did.

CHARLES

Bunch of stuffed shirts— (*He rises, restlessly*) Want another cocktail, Nancy?

NANCY

What good's a cocktail?

CHARLES

I don't know. (*He wanders restlessly toward the hall and looks out*) They're sure giving Barbara a going over. (*He wanders back into the room and stands, thinking*) You know that's true.

NANCY

What is?

CHARLES

I never *did* want to be in the Hawthorn Hill Club. That's not just sour grapes.

NANCY

You tried hard enough to get in.

CHARLES

Yes, I did, didn't I? I wonder why. Why did I do all that to get somewhere I didn't want to be? (*He thinks*) Why have I done a *lot* of things I've done, right from the very start! Do you know there was a time when I wouldn't walk across the street to meet John D. Rockefeller.

NANCY

When was that?

CHARLES

I mean there was a time when I *said* that—when I *felt* it—
and then—(*He pauses, thinking back*)—then from Spruce
Street to Wright-Sherwin to Johnson Street to Boston to New
New to the Stuyvesant Bank—drive, drive, drive—"Yes, sir."
"No, sir." "Polish your apple, sir." Why? What was I trying
to do?

NANCY

What everyone tries to do. Get on.

CHARLES

No, that's not the whole answer.—Nancy, I haven't had
the chance to talk to you since I got back—but remember
what you said you wanted me to do? Get Jessica Lovell—
Clyde—all of it out of my system?

NANCY

Yes.

CHARLES

Well, they're out, Nancy. Going back there—and now losing the job—has certainly kicked them out once and for all.
From the time I first kissed Jessica Lovell in that damned
wallpaper room—that's where it all started. That's where I
started to creep. I think all my life I've been the Spruce
Street boy trying to creep up to Johnson Street.

NANCY

You married me. That didn't get you much farther.

CHARLES

That's what saved me, Nancy. That's what saved me. But it wasn't just Jessica Lovell. It was everything back there. Clyde—my father—and Mr. Lovell—that old bastard . . .

NANCY

(*With a look to where the* BURTONS *went off*)
Charley . . .

CHARLES

That's where it started. That's where the ass forgot everything else and started following the bundle of hay. (*He stops*) Well, to hell with the hay. We'll live. The main thing is I don't have to try to beat the system any more. We're out of it, Nancy. (*Pause.* NANCY *is watching him. He grins*) You know, I feel good. I mean really good—I mean strong, independent—like being able to tell somebody to go to hell. I'm free, Nancy—I'm free to—to—I'm free to read Boswell's *Life of Johnson,* if I want to. Doesn't it make sense to you, Nancy?

NANCY

I don't see why you can't read Boswell—or not join the Hawthorn Hill Club . . .

CHARLES

No, no, Nancy—you don't understand—it's not just the Hawthorn Hill Club, it's a whole way of life! Why, if I told

Tony I didn't want to join the Hawthorn Hill Club . . .
Good Lord, I'd practically be telling him to go to hell. But
as it is now—I'm free—inside. (*He kneels and looks at her*)
Don't you get it, Nance?

NANCY

I don't know.

CHARLES

I'm going to say now what you wouldn't let me say before.
We *have* got each other—*and* the children—*and* we're alive—
and I'm going to try to buy Bill that boat *anyway*. See, Nance?
See?

NANCY

You can't make me feel *glad* we've lost the job, Charley—
but—maybe it's not the world-crushing tragedy I thought it
was. And anyway, you said one wonderfully sweet thing.

CHARLES

What was that?

NANCY

That—marrying me—saved you.

CHARLES

It *did*, Nance. It *did*.

NANCY

And—as you say—we *have* got each other—maybe more
now than before. We damn well better.

CHARLES

Oh, Nancy, you're a funny one.
(*He bends down and kisses her.*)

BURTON

(*Offstage*)

You know, Althea, I think Barbara sounded rather English.

MRS. BURTON

Yes, she has a lovely telephone voice.
(NANCY *and* CHARLES *break off quickly.* CHARLES *takes her hand.*)

CHARLES

Now don't worry about the rest of the evening. We'll all
get along swell now.

BURTON

(*Offstage*)

I'm not sure I like that.
(*The* BURTONS *enter.* NANCY *rises.*)

CHARLES

How's Barbara?

MRS. BURTON

She's fine. Oh, dear, I'm sorry—this has all been terribly
rude . . .

BURTON

You see, we're so anxious about Barbara. She hasn't liked
several schools she's been to lately—but I really think Sarah
Lawrence is going to turn out all right.

CHARLES

Good! How about another cocktail before we go in, Tony?

BURTON

Oh, I've had . . .

CHARLES

Come along. I'm going to have another. This is Friday
night . . .

BURTON

Well—I don't mind if I do. (*He rubs his hands together as*
CHARLES *mixes the cocktail*) You know, it's really cozy here.
I like it. (*He hesitates*) Charley, there's something I want to
ask you. I guess it's all right, here in the bosom of the family.
What do you think of Roger Blakesley?
　　　(*There is a sudden dead pause.* NANCY *looks up at him,*
　　　quickly. CHARLES *turns slowly.*)

CHARLES
(*Casually*)

Why Roger's okay.

BURTON

No, now, we're all alone here. You can speak frankly. The
women won't say anything. Do you like him or don't you?

CHARLES
(*After a moment*)

I think Roger is conscientious, energetic, and well trained,
but I can't say I like him much. Why should I?

BURTON

I rather like him. He's been on my conscience lately. He's so anxious, so much on his toes. He's always in there trying.

CHARLES

I don't know what else you could expect. I've been trying pretty hard myself.

BURTON

Not in the same way, Charley. You're subtler. You're developed, you've matured. Of course, I'm out of touch with things, being where I am, but I've been getting an idea—and maybe I'm entirely wrong. You're in more of a position to know than I am. It seems to me that Blakesley has some idea that we're considering him for that vice-presidency vacancy. Do you know anything about this, Charles?

(NANCY *looks at* CHARLES.)

NANCY

What did Blakesley think you were considering him for?

BURTON

That vice-presidency vacancy. I hadn't given it much thought until the other day when we were talking about your going up to Clyde. But Roger said a few things—and I got to thinking back and—well, when anyone gets ideas like that it's a problem to know what to do with him later. (*He looks at* CHARLES, *suddenly*) *You* never thought any of us were considering Blakesley, did you, Charles?

CHARLES

Why, yes, Tony, I did.

BURTON
(*Astonished*)
Good Lord! (*He looks at* NANCY) You *did?*

NANCY
Now that you mention it, I think it did cross our minds.

BURTON
You amaze me! Roger is quite useful, but he's not the right material at all. Your name comes up before the directors on Monday. I've spoken to them, of course. There won't be any trouble.

CHARLES
Thanks, Tony—that's—that's fine . . .

BURTON
That's what I meant when I said before—now that we'll be working together more closely, I hope we'll all be friends.

CHARLES
Well, here we are.

BURTON
I can hardly believe you didn't realize this, Charley.

CHARLES
I guess when you have a job you really never know where you stand, do you?

BURTON
(*Looking at him, keenly*)
I have the curious feeling that you don't seem overly elated about this, Charley.

CHARLES
(*Quickly*)
I'm sorry. I didn't mean to give that impression. It's just that—I'm a little confused.

BURTON
There's nothing to be confused about. The job is yours. A week from Saturday there'll be a little dinner. You'll be called on to make a few remarks. And oh, yes, I've taken the liberty of putting your name up for membership in the Hawthorn Hill Club. So many of us are there. I hope you don't mind. (*A moment's pause*) I don't think I understand your attitude. You want the job, don't you?

CHARLES
Tony, please don't think I'm ungrateful. It's what I've been working toward all my life, I suppose. But a few minutes ago Nancy and I thought we weren't going to get it—and—curiously enough—I never felt better. And now—suddenly—I feel —well, a little like that time at Dartmouth when I won the half-mile at Freshman track. A little dull—a little tired and a little curious why I ran so hard.

BURTON
We all run hard to win. None of us wants to come in second.

CHARLES

No, I suppose so. And I did run like hell.

BURTON

You know, of course, Charley, that you're really obligated
to take the job. You owe it to us. The bank has invested a
lot of time in you. Besides, this is the natural step in
your life—it's the logical outcome—you can't change a line
of it.

CHARLES

No, that's probably true. And I don't want to change a line
of it. It's just that—well, I suppose nothing you ever work
hard for turns out exactly as you thought it would.

BURTON

We've all felt that. I know I have. Sometimes you half resent
success. But you can't turn back now, Charley. It's too late.

CHARLES

That's true, isn't it? Tony, don't think I don't want the job.
It means a lot to us. And I'm glad you want me. It's just
that—from here on in—I want to be myself. The rest of my
life I want to walk straight up and down—this way—vertical.
I don't want to creep any more—I don't want to ever polish
another apple—I—Tony, I've got to tell you this. I don't want
to join the Hawthorn Hill Club.

BURTON

Really? Why not?

CHARLES

I don't like it.

BURTON

I've always liked the Hawthorn Hill Club.

CHARLES

That's fair enough, Tony. I never have.

BURTON

Well—you certainly must know I wouldn't try to dictate your club to you, Charley. In fact, I've never felt I could dictate to you at all.
(*A moment's pause. The maid enters and nods to* NANCY, *who rises.*)

CHARLES

Well, I guess that means Junior can go to Exeter.

MRS. BURTON

Charles, I see you're reading Boswell's *Life of Johnson*. You know, Nancy, I tried to read it once. It's the dullest thing I ever got into.

NANCY

Oh, no! Don't tell him that!

MRS. BURTON

I wonder if anyone ever really read it through.

CHARLES

I doubt it. I very much doubt it.
(NANCY *and* MR. BURTON *are offstage.* MRS. BURTON *is off and as* CHARLES *starts off:*)

NANCY'S VOICE

Charley, bring some cigarettes.
(*He turns back into the room.* NANCY *enters.*)

NANCY

Charley, never mind the cigarettes.
(*She goes to him and kisses him.*)

CHARLES

What's that for?

NANCY

That's for free.
(*They start off.*)

Curtain